gluten-free
Baking

Publications International, Ltd.

Pictured on the front cover: Apple Pie *(page 136)*
Pictured on the back cover *(left to right):* Double Chocolate Brownies *(page 96)* and Lemon Poppy Seed Muffins *(page 36).*

Photography on pages 7 and 8 by Shutterstock.

ISBN: 978-1-4508-8459-4

Library of Congress Control Number: 2013957950

Manufactured in China.

8 7 6 5 4 3 2 1

Microwave Cooking: Microwave ovens vary in wattage. Use the cooking times as guidelines and check for doneness before adding more time.

Note: This publication is only intended to provide general information. The information is specifically not intended to be a substitute for medical diagnosis or treatment by your physician or other health care professional. You should always consult your own physician or other health care professionals about any medical questions, diagnosis, or treatment. (Products vary among manufacturers. Please check labels carefully to confirm that the products you use are free of gluten.) Not all recipes in this book are appropriate for all people with celiac disease, gluten intolerance, food allergies or sensitivities.

The information obtained by you from this book should not be relied upon for any personal, nutritional, or medical decision. You should consult an appropriate professional for specific advice tailored to your specific situation. PIL makes no representations or warranties, express or implied, with respect to your use of this information.

In no event shall PIL, its affiliates or advertisers be liable for any direct, indirect, punitive, incidental, special, or consequential damages, or any damages whatsoever including, without limitation, damages for personal injury, death, damage to property, or loss of profits, arising out of or in any way connected with the use of any of the above-referenced information or otherwise arising out of the use of this book.

Publications International, Ltd.

Table of Contents

BAKING GLUTEN-FREE AND EASY

There's no need to give away your old cookbooks and recipe cards. Many recipes don't have any problematic ingredients or can easily be converted. When small quantities of flour are needed—for example, to bread chicken or fish or dusting pans or work surfaces—you can substitute any gluten-free flour for regular flour.

Baked goods, especially breads, are a whole lot trickier. While it is certainly possible to buy premade GF cookies, cakes and breads, they are expensive and can't compete with homemade treats. Fortunately, it is possible to turn out luscious gluten-free brownies, cakes, pies and even bread with the recipes in this book and a bit of practice. In fact, warm GF bread from your oven is probably tastier and better for you than most supermarket wheat breads!

Flour Power

You won't be surprised to learn that the trick to making GF baked goods is finding a way to replace the power of gluten. In order to replicate the structure and texture it provides, you'll need to combine different nonwheat flours and add xanthan gum. While you can buy premade GF all-purpose flour blends as well as mixes for anything from pancakes to chocolate cake, it's helpful to know a little about the actual flours in them. It seems there are new choices available every day—hemp flour and pea flour are two of the latest.

Here are descriptions of some of the more common ones.

Almond Flour has a sweet, nutty flavor that complements cookies and cakes. You can make your own almond flour by pulverizing blanched nuts in a food processor. It is very easy to end up with almond butter, though, so beware! Almond flour is low in carbohydrates and high in protein. It is a classic ingredient in Passover cooking.

Chickpea Flour is also called garbanzo flour or besan flour. This hearty flour is high in protein, fiber and calcium. You'll find it in many Indian, Italian and Mediterranean recipes and it is an excellent addition to flour blends.

Coconut Flour is low in carbohydrates and high in fiber. It has a subtle coconut fragrance and flavor. Coconut flour absorbs a lot of liquid and can easily become dense. Recipes usually call for a small amount of coconut flour and more eggs than usual.

Corn Flour is the finely ground form of cornmeal. Masa harina, which is milled from hominy (corn treated with slaked lime) is a special kind of corn flour used to make tortillas and in other Mexican recipes. There is also a special corn flour which is precooked and labeled masarepa or masa al instante.

Cornmeal comes in a variety of grinds and colors, from fine to coarse, and in white, yellow and even blue! It's perfect for corn muffins, polenta and breading  among other things. Cornmeal is nutritious and has a nutty, sweet flavor. Using too coarse a grind can produce gritty baked goods.

Cornstarch has probably always been in your pantry. A fine white powder, cornstarch is highly refined and used  as a thickener and a bland ingredient that lightens many GF flour blends.

Millet Flour is made from a cereal grain that is used in African and Indian cuisine. (Whole millet is also used as bird food!) It is mild in flavor  and easy to digest. Millet's mild flavor, plus a high fiber and protein content make it work well in blends for yeast breads.

Rice Flour (white or brown) is the most commonly used gluten-free flour and a good one-to-one substitute in recipes that only call for a tablespoon or two of regular flour.  Like the rice it is made from, brown rice flour is whole grain, so it is nutritionally better, but makes things heavier.

Rice Flour, Sweet can be confusing, since it's sometimes called glutinous rice flour! It does not contain gluten, but is made from short grain "sticky" rice. The Japanese term for this  flour is mochiko since it is used in making mochi (rice cakes). It is an excellent thickener but has little nutritional value.

Sorghum Flour is sometimes called milo or jowar flour, and is a relatively new and very welcome addition to the gluten-free pantry. It is nutritious and high in protein so it works well in flour blends for breads.  Many find the flavor similar to regular wheat flour.

Soy Flour is ground from roasted soybeans. Choose defatted soy flour. Regular soy flour is extremely perishable and prone to rancidity. Soy flour is high in protein, but it has a distinctive "beany" flavor many people don't like.

Tapioca Flour is often labeled tapioca starch. It comes from the root of the cassava (manioc) plant, as do tapioca  pearls used to make pudding, which are processed differently. Tapioca flour gives a bit of chewiness to baked goods and is also an excellent thickener.

Choco-Berry Cake
(page 66)

FLOUR BLENDS AND FRIENDS

Why can't there be a single one-for-one substitute for wheat flour? Unfortunately wheat flour performs many different functions and is made up of both protein (the gluten) and starches. It helps make pie crusts flaky, cookies chewy and breads crusty. There is no one GF flour that can recreate all those benefits, but with two basic flour blends in your refrigerator, you can turn out yummy cakes, cookies and even yeast breads. Here are the blends used for many of the recipes in this book.

GLUTEN-FREE ALL-PURPOSE FLOUR BLEND
(This blend is for all baked goods not made with yeast.)

1 cup white rice flour
1 cup sorghum flour
1 cup tapioca flour
1 cup cornstarch
1 cup almond flour or coconut flour

Combine all ingredients in a large bowl. Whisk to make sure the flours are evenly distributed. The recipe can be doubled or tripled. Store in an airtight container in the refrigerator. Makes about 5 cups.

GLUTEN-FREE FLOUR BLEND FOR BREADS
(This blend is for recipes that call for yeast.)

1 cup brown rice flour
1 cup sorghum flour
¾ cup millet flour*
1 cup tapioca flour
1 cup cornstarch
⅓ cup instant mashed potato flakes (unflavored)

*If millet flour is not available, chickpea flour may be substituted.

Combine all ingredients in a large bowl. Whisk to make sure flours are evenly distributed. The recipe can be doubled or tripled. Store in an airtight container in the refrigerator. Makes about 5 cups.

Fiber Factoids

Most of us don't get enough fiber in our diets. Here's a list of some common GF flours and their fiber content, from high to low.

FLOUR
FIBER PER 1 CUP

Flour	Fiber per 1 cup	
Chickpea flour	20.9	grams
Almond flour	14.7	grams
Millet flour	10.3	grams
Brown rice flour	7.3	grams
White rice flour	3.8	grams
Cornstarch	1.2	grams
Tapioca	0	grams

BLENDING THE RULES

While gluten-free flour blends may seem mysterious at first, they do follow certain rules. Basic all-purpose flour blends usually start with two parts of grain flour (rice, sorghum or millet), two parts of starch (cornstarch or tapioca flour) and one part of protein flour (a bean or nut). There are many other considerations like flavor and nutrition. While a blend made of white rice flour and cornstarch might work, it wouldn't contain much in the way of fiber, protein or vitamins. You can, of course, purchase ready-made blends at the supermarket or online, but homemade is certainly cheaper and also fresher and better tasting.

STORING AND USING GF FLOUR BLENDS

Most gluten-free flour blends should be stored in the refrigerator or freezer since they contain perishable whole grain or nut flours. Invest in canisters or use clearly marked resealable freezer bags. Bring flours to room temperature before using and remember to rewhisk or shake them so that they are completely combined.

Measuring GF blends is no different than measuring wheat flour, but it is even more important to be accurate. Never

pack flour into a measuring cup. Don't dip the measuring cup into the flour, either, since that can compact it. Fluff the flour and spoon it into the cup. Level off the top with the back of a knife.

BAKING TIPS AND TRICKS

Gluten-free baking isn't harder, it's just different. The good/bad news is that you'll probably be doing more baking now that you're gluten-free. That's good because you won't be eating all of the questionable ingredients in most packaged breads and cookies. The bad news is that you'll have to find the time. There is a bit of a learning curve to gluten-free baking, so don't

be discouraged by a failure. Remember, you probably failed at traditional baking a few times, too! Many products that may not look as beautiful as you would like will still taste very good. You can also turn a total failure into gluten-free crumbs to be used another time.

Mixing Mastery

Gather all the flours you'll need to make a blend and get out your largest bowl.

Many flours, especially the starchy ones, look alike. Pay close attention and check off each ingredient as you go. Blend the flours thoroughly with a whisk.

Don't Gum Things Up!

If you use a store-bought flour blend, be sure to check the ingredients. Some contain xanthan or guar gum already. You do not want to double the amount of gum in a recipe. The recipes in this book assume that you are using a blend WITHOUT xanthan or guar gum.

THINK DIFFERENT

Many batters and doughs look drastically different from their gluten-containing counterparts. They tend to be wetter and stickier. Bread dough is more like a thick, stretchy batter. You can celebrate the fact that you'll never need to knead GF bread dough. That's a good thing, since it's so sticky you'd never be able to! You will need to learn to shape sticky dough by using damp hands or a well-oiled spoon or spatula. Parchment paper can be a real help for lining pans and transporting soft doughs.

You will be using xanthan gum to provide elasticity and hold doughs together. It's important to measure it very carefully. Too much and your baked goods will shrink after baking and you may find a dense, gummy layer of dough near the bottom of the pan.

SMARTY PANS

Pans are a critical part of the recipe. Black or dark metal pans can be a problem because they absorb heat more quickly. The recipes in this book were tested in pans and on baking sheets with light, shiny surfaces. If you must use dark pans, try lining them with foil, watch carefully and lower oven temperatures or cooking times, if necessary. Disposable aluminum pans work surprisingly well for many recipes.

Pan size can be the difference between a perfect cake or loaf and a flop—literally! The same batter intended for a 9×5-inch loaf pan can puff up over the top of an 8×4-inch pan and then collapse. Measure pan size across the top from inside edge to inside edge.

TEMPERAMENTAL TEMPERATURES

Oven temperatures are also important. If you don't have an oven thermometer, you may want to get one. Home ovens are frequently off by as much as 50 degrees. While you're at it, pick up an inexpensive instant-read thermometer, too. It's a big help in knowing when bread is done (190° to 200°F). Gluten-free goods tend to brown more quickly. They can look done on the outside when they're still gooey in the center, so be ready to cover breads or cakes with a sheet of foil to prevent burning.

TROUBLE-SHOOTING

Problem: The cake looked gorgeous when it came out of the oven, but it fell in the center and got mushy.

Solution: Gluten-free baked goods need to be removed from pans quickly or the residual steam can cause them to collapse. Remove them from the pan to a wire rack 5 minutes after they come out of the oven.

Cake left in a hot pan too long can collapse.

Problem: The muffins collapsed over the top of the pan.

Solution: There may have been too much liquid in the batter. Gluten-free flours absorb less liquid than wheat flour.

Too much liquid can make muffins collapse.

Problem: The bread was dry and hard the next morning.

Solution: GF breads stale very quickly. Always keep them well wrapped once they're cool and store in the refrigerator or freezer.

Problem: The bread was burned outside but raw in the middle.

Solution: Try lowering the oven temperature by 25 degrees. Don't bake GF breads in black, glass or nonstick-coated pans. If the outside is browning too fast, cover the bread with foil.

Without xanthan gum, baked goods crumble.

Problem: The cookies crumbled!

Solution: Did you remember the xanthan gum? Without it GF flours lack the elasticity to hold regular baked goods together

Problem: The bread was tough.

Solution: Beating dough for several minutes can lighten it by beating in air. Be sure to beat for the time called for in the recipe. Using a heavy-duty stand mixer may help as well. You may also need to reduce the amount of flour.

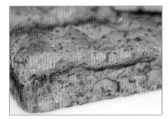

Don't let bread rise higher than the top of the pan, or it will slump.

Problem: The bread looked gorgeous when it came out of the oven, but then it leaned over and folded.

Solution: Don't let your GF bread rise higher than the top of the pan and don't use too small a pan.

Best Breads

Sandwich Bread

MAKES 1 LOAF

3 cups Gluten-Free Flour Blend for Breads (page 6), plus additional for pan
2 packages (¼ ounce each) active dry yeast
2 teaspoons xanthan gum
1 teaspoon salt
1 cup warm water (110°F), plus additional as needed
2 eggs
¼ cup vegetable oil
1 tablespoon honey
1 teaspoon cider vinegar

1. Line 9×5-inch loaf pan with foil, dull side out. (Do not use glass loaf pan.) Extend sides of foil 3 inches up from top of pan. Spray with nonstick cooking spray; dust with flour blend.

2. Combine 3 cups flour blend, yeast, xanthan gum and salt in large bowl. Whisk 1 cup water, eggs, oil, honey and vinegar in medium bowl. Beat into flour mixture with electric mixer at low speed until batter is smooth, shiny and thick. Add additional water by tablespoonfuls if needed. Beat at medium-high speed 5 minutes, scraping bowl occasionally.

3. Spoon batter into prepared pan. Cover with lightly greased plastic wrap. Let rise in warm place 30 minutes or until batter reaches top of pan.

4. Preheat oven to 375°F. Bake 30 to 35 minutes or until bread sounds hollow when tapped and internal temperature is 200°F. Remove to wire rack to cool completely.

Orange-Lemon Citrus Bread

MAKES 1 LOAF

1¾ cups Gluten-Free All-Purpose Flour Blend (page 6),* plus additional for pan
¾ cup sugar
1 tablespoon plus ½ teaspoon grated lemon peel, divided
2 teaspoons baking powder
1 teaspoon xanthan gum
¼ teaspoon salt
1 cup milk
½ cup vegetable oil
1 egg
1 teaspoon vanilla
¼ cup orange marmalade

Or use any all-purpose gluten-free flour blend that does not contain xanthan gum.

1. Preheat oven to 350°F. Spray 9×5-inch loaf pan with nonstick cooking spray; dust with flour blend.

2. Combine 1¾ cups flour blend, sugar, 1 tablespoon lemon peel, baking powder, xanthan gum and salt in large bowl; mix well. Whisk milk, oil, egg and vanilla in small bowl until well blended.

3. Make well in flour mixture; pour in milk mixture and stir just until blended. (Batter will be thin.) Pour into prepared pan.

4. Bake 45 minutes or until toothpick inserted into center comes out clean. Cool in pan on wire rack 5 minutes.

5. Meanwhile, combine marmalade and remaining ½ teaspoon lemon peel in small microwavable bowl. Microwave on HIGH 15 seconds or until slightly melted.

6. Remove bread to wire rack. Spread marmalade mixture evenly over top. Cool completely before serving.

Olive and Herb Focaccia

MAKES 2 FOCACCIA BREADS

3 cups Gluten-Free Flour Blend for Breads (page 6)
2 packages (¼ ounce each) active dry yeast
2 teaspoons xanthan gum
1 teaspoon salt
1¼ cups warm water (110°F), divided
3 egg whites
¼ cup extra virgin olive oil
1 tablespoon honey
1 teaspoon cider vinegar

Toppings

1 cup chopped pitted kalamata olives
3 tablespoons chopped fresh rosemary leaves
2 tablespoons chopped fresh thyme
3 cloves garlic, minced
¼ cup extra virgin olive oil
   Salt and black pepper
¼ cup grated Romano cheese

1. Combine flour blend, yeast, xanthan gum and 1 teaspoon salt in large bowl. Whisk 1 cup water, egg whites, ¼ cup oil, honey and vinegar in medium bowl until well blended. Beat into flour mixture with electric mixer at low speed until combined. (Batter should be smooth, shiny and thick.) Add additional water, 1 tablespoon at a time, if necessary. Beat at medium-high speed 5 minutes, scraping bowl occasionally.

2. Line pizza pans or baking sheets with parchment paper or foil. Place dough in center of prepared pans. Using wet hands, spread dough into two 8-inch rounds, about ½ inch thick. Let rest 20 minutes. Preheat oven to 450°F.

3. Dimple tops of dough rounds with fingertips or back of wooden spoon. Sprinkle evenly with olives, rosemary, thyme and garlic. Drizzle with ¼ cup oil. Sprinkle with salt and pepper.

4. Bake 15 minutes or until lightly browned. Immediately sprinkle with cheese. Cool slightly on wire rack before slicing.

Chocolate Chip Elvis Bread

MAKES 4 MINI LOAVES

2½ cups Gluten-Free All-Purpose Flour Blend (page 6)*
½ cup granulated sugar
½ cup packed brown sugar
1 tablespoon baking powder
1 teaspoon xanthan gum
¾ teaspoon salt
1 cup mashed ripe bananas (about 2 large)
1 cup rice milk
¾ cup peanut butter
¼ cup vegetable oil
   Prepared powdered egg replacer equal to 1 egg
1 teaspoon vanilla
1 cup semisweet chocolate chips

Or use any all-purpose gluten-free flour blend that does not contain xanthan gum.

1. Preheat oven to 350°F. Spray 4 mini (5½×3-inch) or 2 (8×4-inch) loaf pans with nonstick cooking spray.

2. Combine flour blend, granulated sugar, brown sugar, baking powder, xanthan gum and salt in large bowl; mix well. Beat bananas, rice milk, peanut butter, oil, egg replacer and vanilla in medium bowl until well blended. Add banana mixture and chocolate chips to flour mixture; stir just until moistened. Pour into prepared pans.

3. Bake 40 minutes or until toothpick inserted into centers comes out clean (45 to 50 minutes for 8×4-inch pans). Cool in pans on wire racks 10 minutes. Remove from pans; cool completely on wire racks.

Chili Cheese Bread

MAKES 1 LOAF

¾ cup water
2 eggs
3 tablespoons olive oil
1½ cups Gluten-Free Flour Blend for Breads (page 6)
1 cup (4 ounces) shredded Cheddar cheese
1 tablespoon sugar
1 tablespoon chili powder
1 package (¼ ounce) active dry yeast
1½ teaspoons xanthan gum
1 teaspoon unflavored gelatin
½ teaspoon salt

1. Spray 8×4-inch loaf pan with nonstick cooking spray.

2. Beat water, eggs and oil in large bowl with electric mixer at medium speed until combined. Whisk flour blend, cheese, sugar, chili powder, yeast, xanthan gum, gelatin and salt in large bowl until thoroughly mixed.

3. Gradually beat flour mixture into egg mixture; beat at low speed 10 minutes. Batter will be sticky and stretchy. Spoon batter into prepared pan.

4. Cover and let rise in warm place about 1 hour or until dough almost reaches top of pan.

5. Preheat oven to 350°F. Bake 40 to 50 minutes or until bread sounds hollow when tapped and internal temperature is 190°F. Check after 20 minutes and cover with foil if bread is browning too quickly. Cool in pan on wire rack 10 minutes. Remove from pan; cool completely before slicing.

Cinnamon Raisin Bread

MAKES 1 LOAF

3 cups Gluten-Free Flour Blend for Breads (page 6), plus additional for pan

⅓ cup sugar

1 tablespoon ground cinnamon

2 packages (¼ ounce each) active dry yeast

2 teaspoons xanthan gum

1 teaspoon salt

1¼ cups plus 2 tablespoons warm milk, divided

2 eggs

¼ cup vegetable oil

1 tablespoon honey or maple syrup

1 teaspoon cider vinegar

¾ cup raisins

1 tablespoon gluten-free oats (optional)

1. Line 9×5-inch loaf pan with foil, dull side out. Extend sides of foil 3 inches up from top of pan. Spray with nonstick cooking spray; dust with flour blend.

2. Combine sugar and cinnamon in small bowl; mix well. Set aside.

3. Combine 3 cups flour blend, yeast, xanthan gum and salt in large bowl; mix well. Whisk 1¼ cups warm milk, eggs, oil, honey and vinegar in medium bowl until well blended. Beat milk mixture into flour mixture with electric mixer at low speed until batter is smooth, shiny and thick. Beat at medium-high speed 5 minutes, scraping bowl occasionally. Stir in raisins.

4. Place large sheet of parchment paper on work surface; sprinkle with flour blend. Scoop batter onto center of paper. Using dampened hands or oiled spatula, spread batter into 18×9-inch rectangle. Brush with remaining 2 tablespoons warm milk. Sprinkle evenly with all but 1 tablespoon cinnamon-sugar, leaving 1-inch border.

5. Using parchment paper, roll up dough jelly-roll style, beginning at short end. Push ends in to fit length of pan; trim excess paper. Using parchment paper, lift roll and place in prepared pan. (Leave parchment in pan.) Sprinkle with remaining 1 tablespoon cinnamon-sugar and oats, if desired.

6. Preheat oven to 375°F. Bake 35 to 45 minutes or until bread sounds hollow when tapped and internal temperature is 200°F. Remove bread from pan; remove parchment and foil. Cool completely on wire rack.

Applesauce-Spice Bread

MAKES 9 SERVINGS

1½ cups Gluten-Free All-Purpose Flour Blend (page 6)*
1½ cups unsweetened applesauce
 ¾ cup packed brown sugar
 ½ cup shortening
 1 teaspoon baking soda
 1 teaspoon ground cinnamon
 1 teaspoon vanilla
 ¾ teaspoon xanthan gum
 ½ teaspoon baking powder
 ¼ teaspoon salt
 ¼ teaspoon ground nutmeg
 ½ cup chopped walnuts, toasted**
 ½ cup raisins
    Powdered sugar

Or use any all-purpose gluten-free flour blend that does not contain xanthan gum.

**To toast walnuts, spread in single layer on baking sheet. Bake in preheated 350°F oven 8 to 10 minutes or until golden brown, stirring frequently.*

1. Preheat oven to 350°F. Spray 9-inch square baking pan with nonstick cooking spray.

2. Beat flour blend, applesauce, brown sugar, shortening, baking soda, cinnamon, vanilla, xanthan gum, baking powder, salt and nutmeg in large bowl with electric mixer at low speed 30 seconds. Beat at high speed 3 minutes. Stir in walnuts and raisins. Pour into prepared pan.

3. Bake 30 minutes or until toothpick inserted into center comes out clean. Cool completely in pan on wire rack. Sprinkle with powdered sugar before serving.

Chili Corn Bread

MAKES 12 SERVINGS

2 teaspoons vegetable oil

¼ cup chopped red bell pepper

¼ cup chopped green bell pepper

2 small jalapeño peppers, minced

2 cloves garlic, minced

¾ cup corn

1½ cups yellow cornmeal

½ cup Gluten-Free All-Purpose Flour Blend (page 6)*

2 tablespoons sugar

2 teaspoons baking powder

1½ teaspoons xanthan gum

½ teaspoon baking soda

½ teaspoon salt

½ teaspoon ground cumin

1½ cups low-fat buttermilk

2 egg whites

1 egg

¼ cup (½ stick) butter, melted

*Or use any all-purpose gluten-free flour blend that does not contain xanthan gum.

1. Preheat oven to 375°F. Spray 8-inch square baking pan with nonstick cooking spray.

2. Heat oil in small skillet over medium heat. Add bell peppers, jalapeño peppers and garlic; cook and stir 3 to 4 minutes or until peppers are tender. Stir in corn; cook 1 to 2 minutes. Remove from heat.

3. Combine cornmeal, flour blend, sugar, baking powder, xanthan gum, baking soda, salt and cumin in large bowl. Add buttermilk, egg whites, egg and butter; mix until blended. Stir in corn mixture. Pour into prepared pan.

4. Bake 25 to 30 minutes or until golden brown. Cool completely in pan on wire rack.

Make Some Muffins

Piña Colada Muffins

MAKES 18 MUFFINS

2 cups Gluten-Free All-Purpose Flour Blend (page 6)*
¾ cup sugar
½ cup flaked coconut, plus additional for garnish
1 tablespoon baking powder
1 teaspoon xanthan gum
½ teaspoon baking soda
½ teaspoon salt
2 eggs
1 cup sour cream
1 can (8 ounces) crushed pineapple in juice, undrained
¼ cup (½ stick) butter, melted
⅛ teaspoon coconut extract

*Or use any all-purpose gluten-free flour blend that does not contain xanthan gum.

1. Preheat oven to 400°F. Spray 18 standard (2½-inch) muffin cups with nonstick cooking spray or line with paper baking cups.

2. Combine flour blend, sugar, ½ cup coconut, baking powder, xanthan gum, baking soda and salt in large bowl; mix well.

3. Beat eggs in medium bowl with electric mixer at medium speed 1 to 2 minutes or until frothy. Beat in sour cream, pineapple with juice, butter and coconut extract. Stir into flour mixture just until combined. Spoon batter evenly into prepared muffin cups.

4. Bake 15 to 20 minutes or until toothpick inserted into centers comes out clean. If desired, sprinkle tops of muffins with additional coconut after first 10 minutes of baking. Cool in pans 2 minutes. Remove to wire racks to cool slightly. Serve warm or at room temperature.

Spiced Sweet Potato Muffins

MAKES 12 MUFFINS

⅓ cup plus 2 tablespoons packed brown sugar, divided
2 teaspoons ground cinnamon, divided
1½ cups Gluten-Free All-Purpose Flour Blend (page 6)*
1 tablespoon baking powder
½ teaspoon salt
½ teaspoon baking soda
½ teaspoon xanthan gum
½ teaspoon ground allspice
1 cup mashed cooked or canned sweet potatoes
¾ cup milk
¼ cup vegetable oil
¼ cup unsweetened applesauce

*Or use any all-purpose gluten-free flour blend that does not contain xanthan gum.

1. Preheat oven to 425°F. Line 12 standard (2½-inch) muffin cups with paper baking cups or spray with nonstick cooking spray.

2. Combine 2 tablespoons brown sugar and 1 teaspoon cinnamon in small bowl; mix well. Set aside.

3. Combine flour blend, remaining ⅓ cup brown sugar, baking powder, remaining 1 teaspoon cinnamon, salt, baking soda, xanthan gum and allspice in large bowl; mix well.

4. Combine sweet potatoes, milk, oil and applesauce in medium bowl. Stir into flour mixture just until moistened. Spoon batter evenly into prepared muffin cups. Sprinkle evenly with cinnamon-sugar.

5. Bake 14 to 16 minutes or until toothpick inserted into centers comes out clean. Cool in pan on wire rack 5 minutes. Remove to wire rack to cool slightly. Serve warm or at room temperature.

Blueberry Coconut Flour Muffins

MAKES 12 MUFFINS

6 eggs

½ cup sugar

¼ cup (½ stick) butter, melted

¼ cup whole milk

½ cup plus 2 teaspoons coconut flour,* divided

2 teaspoons grated lemon peel

½ teaspoon salt

½ teaspoon baking powder

½ teaspoon xanthan gum

1 cup blueberries

Coconut flour is a gluten-free, high-fiber flour available in the specialty flour section of many supermarkets. It can also be ordered online.

1. Preheat oven to 375°F. Line 12 standard (2½-inch) muffin cups with paper baking cups.

2. Whisk eggs, sugar, butter and milk in medium bowl until well blended.

3. Mix ½ cup coconut flour, lemon peel, salt, baking powder and xanthan gum in medium bowl. Sift flour mixture into egg mixture. Whisk until smooth.

4. Combine blueberries and remaining 2 teaspoons coconut flour in small bowl. Stir gently into batter. Spoon batter evenly into prepared muffin cups.

5. Bake 12 to 15 minutes or until toothpick inserted into centers comes out clean. Cool in pan on wire rack 5 minutes. Remove to wire rack to cool slightly. Serve warm or at room temperature.

Corn Muffins

MAKES 12 MUFFINS

1 cup Gluten-Free All-Purpose Flour Blend (page 6)*
1 cup cornmeal
½ cup sugar
1½ teaspoons baking powder
1 teaspoon baking soda
½ teaspoon salt
½ teaspoon xanthan gum
1 cup buttermilk
2 eggs
¼ cup (½ stick) butter, melted

*Or use any all-purpose gluten-free flour blend that does not contain xanthan gum.

1. Preheat oven to 350°F. Spray 12 standard (2½-inch) muffin cups with nonstick cooking spray or line with paper baking cups.

2. Combine flour blend, cornmeal, sugar, baking powder, baking soda, salt and xanthan gum in large bowl. Whisk buttermilk, eggs and butter in medium bowl until well blended. Add to flour mixture; mix well. (Batter will be thick.) Spoon batter evenly into prepared muffin cups.

3. Bake 20 to 25 minutes or until lightly browned and toothpick inserted into centers comes out clean. Cool in pan on wire rack 5 minutes. Remove to wire rack to cool slightly. Serve warm or at room temperature.

Applesauce Muffins

MAKES 16 MUFFINS

2 cups Gluten-Free All-Purpose Flour Blend (page 6)*

½ cup plus 3 tablespoons granulated sugar, divided

½ cup plus 3 tablespoons packed brown sugar, divided

4 teaspoons ground cinnamon, divided

2 teaspoons baking powder

1 teaspoon baking soda

1 teaspoon xanthan gum

½ cup chunky applesauce

½ cup vegetable oil

½ cup apple cider

2 eggs

3 tablespoons dairy-free margarine, melted

Powdered sugar

Or use any all-purpose gluten-free flour blend that does not contain xanthan gum.

1. Preheat oven to 350°F. Line 16 standard (2½-inch) muffin cups with paper baking cups.

2. Combine flour blend, ½ cup granulated sugar, ½ cup brown sugar, 3 teaspoons cinnamon, baking powder, baking soda and xanthan gum in large bowl. Stir in applesauce, oil, apple cider and eggs until well blended. Spoon batter evenly into prepared muffin cups.

3. Stir remaining 3 tablespoons granulated sugar, 3 tablespoons brown sugar, 1 teaspoon cinnamon and margarine with fork until small clumps form. Sprinkle evenly over batter.

4. Bake 25 to 30 minutes. Cool in pans on wire racks 5 minutes. Remove to wire racks to cool slightly. Sprinkle with powdered sugar, if desired. Serve warm or at room temperature.

Lemon Poppy Seed Muffins

MAKES 18 MUFFINS

2 cups Gluten-Free All-Purpose Flour Blend (page 6)*

1¼ cups granulated sugar

¼ cup poppy seeds

2 tablespoons plus 2 teaspoons grated lemon peel, divided

1 tablespoon baking powder

¾ teaspoon xanthan gum

½ teaspoon baking soda

½ teaspoon ground cardamom

¼ teaspoon salt

2 eggs

½ cup (1 stick) butter, melted

½ cup milk

½ cup plus 2 tablespoons lemon juice, divided

1 cup powdered sugar

Additional grated lemon peel (optional)

Or use any all-purpose gluten-free flour blend that does not contain xanthan gum.

1. Preheat oven to 400°F. Line 18 standard (2½-inch) muffin cups with paper baking cups or spray with nonstick cooking spray.

2. Combine flour blend, granulated sugar, poppy seeds, 2 tablespoons lemon peel, baking powder, xanthan gum, baking soda, cardamom and salt in large bowl. Beat eggs in medium bowl. Add butter, milk and ½ cup lemon juice; mix well. Stir into flour mixture just until blended. Spoon batter evenly into prepared muffin cups.

3. Bake 15 to 20 minutes or until toothpick inserted into centers comes out clean. Cool in pans on wire racks 10 minutes. Place muffins on sheet of foil or waxed paper.

4. Combine powdered sugar and remaining 2 teaspoons lemon peel in small bowl; stir in enough remaining lemon juice to make pourable glaze. Spoon over muffins. Garnish with additional lemon peel. Serve warm or at room temperature.

Pumpkin Muffins

MAKES 12 MUFFINS

2¼ cups Gluten-Free All-Purpose Flour Blend (page 6)*
½ teaspoon salt
½ teaspoon ground ginger
½ teaspoon ground nutmeg
½ teaspoon xanthan gum
¼ teaspoon baking soda
1 cup packed dark brown sugar
1 cup canned solid-pack pumpkin
½ cup (1 stick) butter, melted and cooled
2 eggs
¼ cup buttermilk
3 tablespoons molasses
1 teaspoon vanilla

*Or use any all-purpose gluten-free flour blend that does not contain xanthan gum.

1. Preheat oven to 400°F. Spray 12 standard (2½-inch) muffin cups with nonstick cooking spray.

2. Combine flour blend, salt, ginger, nutmeg, xanthan gum and baking soda in medium bowl. Whisk brown sugar, pumpkin, butter, eggs, buttermilk, molasses and vanilla in large bowl until well blended. Add flour mixture in two additions, stirring until well blended after each addition. Spoon batter evenly into prepared muffin cups.

3. Bake 18 to 22 minutes or until toothpick inserted into centers comes out clean. Cool in pan on wire rack 5 minutes. Remove to wire rack to cool slightly. Serve warm or at room temperature.

Cornmeal Pecan Muffins

MAKES 12 MUFFINS

1 cup Gluten-Free All-Purpose Flour Blend (page 6)*
1 cup cornmeal
1 cup sugar
1½ teaspoons baking powder
1 teaspoon baking soda
½ teaspoon salt
½ teaspoon xanthan gum
1 cup low-fat buttermilk
2 eggs
¼ cup (½ stick) butter, melted
¼ cup chopped pecans, toasted**

*Or use any all-purpose gluten-free flour blend that does not contain xanthan gum.

**To toast pecans, spread in a single layer on ungreased baking sheet. Bake in preheated 350°F oven 8 to 10 minutes or until fragrant, stirring occasionally.

1. Preheat oven to 350°F. Spray 12 standard (2½-inch) muffin cups with nonstick cooking spray or line with paper baking cups.

2. Combine flour blend, cornmeal, sugar, baking powder, baking soda, salt and xanthan gum in large bowl; mix well. Whisk buttermilk, eggs and butter in medium bowl until well blended. Stir into cornmeal mixture just until moistened. (Batter will be thick.) Fold in pecans. Spoon batter evenly into prepared muffin cups.

3. Bake 18 to 20 minutes or until lightly browned and toothpick inserted into centers comes out clean. Cool in pan on wire rack 5 minutes. Remove to wire rack to cool slightly. Serve warm or at room temperature.

Chocolate Chip Scones

MAKES 18 SCONES

2 cups Gluten-Free All-Purpose Flour Blend (page 6),* plus additional
   for work surface

¼ cup sugar

2½ teaspoons baking powder

¾ teaspoon salt

¾ teaspoon xanthan gum

½ teaspoon baking soda

½ cup (1 stick) cold butter, cut into small pieces

1 cup semisweet chocolate chips, divided

¾ cup milk

½ cup plain yogurt

Or use any all-purpose gluten-free flour blend that does not contain xanthan gum.

1. Preheat oven to 425°F.

2. Combine 2 cups flour blend, sugar, baking powder, salt, xanthan gum and baking soda in large bowl; mix well. Cut butter into flour mixture with pastry blender or two knives until coarse crumbs form. Stir in ½ cup chocolate chips.

3. Whisk milk and yogurt in medium bowl until well blended. Gradually add to flour mixture; stir just until dough begins to form. (You may not need all of yogurt mixture.)

4. Transfer dough to floured surface. Knead five to six times or until dough forms. Divide into three pieces. Pat each piece into circle about ½ inch thick. Cut each circle into six wedges using floured knife. Place 2 inches apart on ungreased baking sheets.

5. Bake 10 to 14 minutes or until lightly browned. Remove to wire rack.

6. Meanwhile, place remaining ½ cup chocolate chips in small resealable food storage bag; seal bag. Microwave on HIGH at 30-second intervals until chocolate is melted. Knead bag until smooth. Cut off tiny corner of bag; drizzle chocolate over scones. Let stand until set.

Brazilian Cheese Rolls (Pão de Queijo)

MAKES ABOUT 20 ROLLS

1 cup whole milk
¼ cup (½ stick) butter, cut into pieces
¼ cup vegetable oil
2 cups plus 2 tablespoons tapioca flour*
2 eggs
1 cup grated Parmesan cheese or other firm cheese

Sometimes labeled tapioca starch.

1. Preheat oven to 350°F.

2. Combine milk, butter and oil in large saucepan. Bring to a boil over medium heat, stirring to melt butter. Once mixture reaches a boil, remove from heat. Stir in tapioca flour. Mixture will be thick and stretchy.

3. Stir in eggs, one at a time, and cheese. Mixture will be very stiff. Cool in pan until easy to handle.

4. Roll heaping tablespoonfuls of dough into 1½-inch balls with tapioca-floured hands. Place about 1 inch apart on ungreased baking sheet.

5. Bake 20 to 25 minutes or until puffed and golden. Serve warm.

Note: These moist, chewy rolls are a Brazilian specialty and are always made with tapioca flour instead of wheat flour. In Brazil they are popular at breakfast, lunch or dinner.

Sweet Cherry Biscuits

MAKES ABOUT 10 BISCUITS

2 cups gluten-free biscuit baking mix, plus additional for work surface
¼ cup sugar
2 teaspoons baking powder
½ teaspoon salt
½ teaspoon crushed dried rosemary
½ cup (1 stick) butter, cut into small pieces
¾ cup milk
½ cup dried cherries, chopped

1. Preheat oven to 425°F.

2. Combine 2 cups baking mix, sugar, baking powder, salt and rosemary in large bowl. Cut in butter with pastry blender or two knives until coarse crumbs form. Stir in milk to form sticky dough. Fold in cherries.

3. Pat dough to 1-inch thickness on surface lightly dusted with baking mix. Cut out circles with 3-inch biscuit cutter. Place 1 inch apart on ungreased baking sheet.

4. Bake 15 minutes or until golden brown. Cool on wire rack 5 minutes; serve warm.

tip Serve these sweet biscuits with jam and butter for breakfast or an after-school snack

Cinnamon Scones

MAKES 12 SCONES

2 cups Gluten-Free All-Purpose Flour Blend (page 6),* plus additional
   for work surface
¼ cup sugar
2½ teaspoons baking powder
¾ teaspoon salt
¾ teaspoon xanthan gum
½ teaspoon baking soda
½ cup (1 stick) cold butter, cut into small pieces
⅓ cup cinnamon chips
¾ cup whole milk
½ cup plain yogurt
2 tablespoons cinnamon-sugar

Or use any all-purpose gluten-free flour blend that does not contain xanthan gum.

1. Preheat oven to 425°F.

2. Combine 2 cups flour blend, sugar, baking powder, salt, xanthan gum and baking soda in large bowl. Cut in butter with pastry blender or two knives until coarse crumbs form. Add cinnamon chips; toss to combine.

3. Whisk milk and yogurt in medium bowl until well blended. Gradually add to flour mixture, stirring just until dough begins to form. (You may not need all of yogurt mixture.)

4. Transfer dough to floured surface. Knead five to six times until dough forms. Divide dough into two pieces. Pat each piece into 5-inch circle, about ½ inch thick. Cut each circle into six wedges using floured knife. Place 2 inches apart on ungreased baking sheet. Sprinkle with cinnamon-sugar.

5. Bake 10 to 14 minutes or until lightly browned. Remove to wire rack to cool slightly. Serve warm or at room temperature.

Tip: To make cinnamon-sugar, combine 2 tablespoons sugar and ½ tablespoon ground cinnamon in a small bowl; mix well.

Arepas (Latin American Corn Cakes)

MAKES 6 TO 8 AREPAS

1½ cups instant corn flour for arepas*
½ teaspoon salt
1½ to 2 cups hot water (120°F)
⅓ cup shredded Mexican cheese blend
1 tablespoon butter, melted

*This flour is also called masarepa, masa al instante and harina precodica. It is not the same as masa harina or regular cornmeal. Purchase arepa flour at Latin American markets or online.

1. Preheat oven to 350°F. Combine instant corn flour and salt in medium bowl. Stir in 1½ cups hot water. Dough should be smooth and moist but not sticky; add more water, 1 tablespoon at a time, if necessary. Add cheese and butter. Knead until dough is consistency of smooth mashed potatoes.

2. Lightly grease heavy skillet or griddle; heat over medium heat. Divide dough into six to eight equal pieces; flatten and pat dough into 4-inch discs ½ inch thick. (If dough cracks or is too dry, return to bowl and add additional water, 1 tablespoon at a time.)

3. Immediately place dough pieces in hot skillet. Cook 3 to 5 minutes per side or until browned in spots. Remove to baking sheet.

4. Bake 15 minutes or until arepas sound hollow when tapped. Serve warm.

Arepa Breakfast Sandwiches: Split arepas by piercing edges with fork as you would English muffins. Fill with scrambled eggs, cheese and salsa.

tip Freeze leftover arepas in airtight freezer food storage bags.

Corn and Sunflower Seed Biscuits

MAKES 12 BISCUITS

2 cups gluten-free biscuit baking mix

1 tablespoon sugar

2 teaspoons baking powder

½ teaspoon salt

½ teaspoon dried thyme

5 tablespoons dairy-free margarine

1 cup rice milk

1 cup corn*

⅓ cup plus 6 teaspoons salted roasted sunflower seeds, divided

*Use fresh or thawed frozen corn; do not use supersweet corn.

1. Preheat oven to 400°F. Line baking sheet with parchment paper or spray with nonstick cooking spray.

2. Combine baking mix, sugar, baking powder, salt and thyme in large bowl. Cut in margarine with pastry blender or two knives until mixture resembles coarse crumbs. Add rice milk; stir gently to form soft sticky dough. Stir in corn and ⅓ cup sunflower seeds. Drop dough by ¼ cupfuls onto prepared baking sheet. Sprinkle ½ teaspoon sunflower seeds on each biscuit.

3. Bake 18 to 20 minutes or until biscuits are golden. Remove to wire rack to cool slightly. Serve warm.

Apricot Cranberry Scones

MAKES ABOUT 15 SCONES

2 cups Gluten-Free All-Purpose Flour Blend (page 6),* plus additional
    for work surface
¼ cup sugar
2½ teaspoons baking powder
¾ teaspoon salt
¾ teaspoon xanthan gum
½ teaspoon baking soda
½ cup (1 stick) cold butter, cut into small pieces
¼ cup chopped dried apricots
¼ cup dried cranberries
¾ cup milk
½ cup plain yogurt

*Or use any all-purpose gluten-free flour blend that does not contain xanthan gum.

1. Preheat oven to 425°F.

2. Combine 2 cups flour blend, sugar, baking powder, salt, xanthan gum and baking
soda in large bowl. Cut in butter with pastry blender or two knives until coarse crumbs
form. Add apricots and cranberries; toss to combine.

3. Whisk milk and yogurt in medium bowl until well blended. Gradually add to flour
mixture, stirring just until dough forms. (You may not need all of yogurt mixture.)

4. Transfer dough to floured surface. Knead five to six times until dough forms. Pat
dough into circle about ½ inch thick. Cut into 2-inch circles with floured biscuit cutter.
Place 2 inches apart on ungreased baking sheet. Press together remaining dough and
cut additional scones.

5. Bake 10 to 14 minutes or until lightly browned. Remove to wire rack to cool slightly.
Serve warm or at room temperature.

Yogurt Chive Biscuits

MAKES 12 BISCUITS

2 cups gluten-free biscuit baking mix
1 tablespoon sugar
½ teaspoon salt
¼ teaspoon dried oregano
¼ cup (½ stick) cold butter, cut into pieces
1 cup plain Greek yogurt
½ cup whole milk
½ cup finely chopped fresh chives

1. Preheat oven to 400°F. Line baking sheet with parchment paper or spray with nonstick cooking spray.

2. Combine baking mix, sugar, salt and oregano in large bowl. Cut in butter with pastry blender or two knives until coarse crumbs form. Add yogurt and milk; stir gently to form soft sticky dough. Stir in chives. Drop dough by ¼ cupfuls onto prepared baking sheet.

3. Bake 15 to 16 minutes or until light golden brown. Remove to wire rack to cool slightly. Serve warm.

Cakes and Cheesecakes

Summer Fruit Brunch Cake

MAKES 6 SERVINGS

¾ cup Gluten-Free All-Purpose Flour Blend (page 6)*

½ cup cornmeal

1 teaspoon xanthan gum

½ teaspoon baking powder

¼ teaspoon baking soda

⅔ cup sugar

½ cup (1 stick) dairy-free margarine, softened

2 eggs

½ cup vanilla soy yogurt, plus additional for topping

1 cup fresh peach slices *or* 1 can (about 15 ounces) sliced peaches in juice, drained

Sliced strawberries

Or use any gluten-free all-purpose flour blend that does not contain xanthan gum.

1. Preheat oven to 325°F. Spray 9-inch pie plate with nonstick cooking spray. Combine flour blend, cornmeal, xanthan gum, baking powder and baking soda in medium bowl.

2. Beat sugar and margarine in large bowl with electric mixer at medium speed until fluffy. Add eggs and ½ cup yogurt; beat until well blended. Beat in flour mixture at low speed until combined. Stir in peaches. Pour batter into prepared pie plate.

3. Bake 35 minutes or until toothpick inserted into center comes out clean. Top with strawberries and drizzle with additional yogurt.

Lemon Cheesecake

MAKES 10 TO 12 SERVINGS

Crust
5 tablespoons butter, softened
¼ cup sugar
1½ teaspoons grated lemon peel
1 cup Gluten-Free All-Purpose Flour Blend (page 6)*
1 teaspoon xanthan gum
⅛ teaspoon salt

Filling
1 package (2¾ teaspoons) unflavored gelatin
¼ cup water
12 ounces cream cheese, softened
¾ cup sugar
⅓ cup lemon juice
1 cup whipping cream, at room temperature

Topping
¼ cup sugar
2 egg yolks
1 egg
3 tablespoons lemon juice
⅛ teaspoon salt
3 tablespoons butter
Grated lemon peel (optional)

*Or use any all-purpose gluten-free flour blend that does not contain xanthan gum.

1. Preheat oven to 350°F. Line 9-inch springform pan with foil or parchment paper; spray with nonstick cooking spray.

2. For crust, beat 5 tablespoons butter, ¼ cup sugar and 1½ teaspoons lemon peel in large bowl with electric mixer at medium speed 1 minute or until light and fluffy. Beat in flour blend, xanthan gum and ⅛ teaspoon salt at low speed until mixture resembles coarse crumbs. Press mixture onto bottom of prepared pan. Bake 10 to 12 minutes or until golden brown. Cool completely in pan on wire rack.

continued on page 62

3. Meanwhile for filling, sprinkle gelatin over water in small microwavable bowl. Let stand 5 minutes or until gelatin softens. Microwave on HIGH 30 seconds or until gelatin is dissolved and mixture bubbles around edge.

4. Beat cream cheese and ¾ cup sugar in large bowl with electric mixer at medium-high speed until well blended. Beat in ⅓ cup lemon juice at low speed. Add cream; beat at medium-high speed 2 minutes or until fluffy, scraping sides of bowl as necessary. Add gelatin; beat 3 minutes or until well combined. Pour mixture over crust. Cover and refrigerate until set.

5. For topping, combine ¼ cup sugar, egg yolks, egg, 3 tablespoons lemon juice and ⅛ teaspoon salt in small saucepan; cook and stir over medium-low heat 5 minutes or until thickened. Remove from heat.

6. Stir in 3 tablespoons butter until well blended and butter is melted. Pour mixture through fine-mesh sieve into medium bowl. Let stand 5 minutes to cool slightly.

7. Spread cooled lemon topping over cheesecake. Cover and refrigerate 4 hours or until set. Garnish with lemon peel.

Flower Power Strawberry Cake

MAKES 12 SERVINGS

1 package (15 ounces) gluten-free yellow cake mix
1 container (6 ounces) strawberry soy yogurt
3 eggs
⅓ cup vegetable oil
1 package (4-serving size) strawberry gelatin
1 container (16 ounces) dairy-free white or vanilla frosting
12 medium strawberries

1. Preheat oven to 350°F. Lightly grease 9-inch square baking pan.

2. Beat cake mix, yogurt, eggs, oil and gelatin in large bowl with electric mixer at low speed about 1 minute or until blended. Increase speed to medium; beat 1 to 2 minutes or until smooth. Spread batter in prepared pan.

3. Bake 38 to 43 minutes or until toothpick inserted into center comes out clean. Cool completely in pan on wire rack.

4. Frost and decorate with strawberry wedges to make flowers.

Chocolate Marble Praline Cheesecake

MAKES 12 TO 16 SERVINGS

Crust

2 cups gluten-free shortbread cookie crumbs
½ cup finely chopped toasted pecans*
6 tablespoons (¾ stick) butter, melted
¼ cup powdered sugar

Cheesecake

3 packages (8 ounces each) cream cheese, softened
1¼ cups packed brown sugar
3 eggs, lightly beaten
½ cup sour cream
1½ teaspoons vanilla
1 square (1 ounce) unsweetened chocolate, melted
20 to 25 pecan halves (½ cup)
Gluten-free caramel ice cream topping

*To toast pecans, spread in a single layer on ungreased baking sheet. Bake in preheated 350°F oven 8 to 10 minutes or until fragrant, stirring occasionally.

1. Preheat oven to 350°F.

2. Combine cookie crumbs, chopped pecans, butter and powdered sugar in food processor; pulse until combined. Press onto bottom and up side of ungreased 9-inch springform pan. Bake 10 to 15 minutes or until lightly browned. Cool completely on wire rack.

3. Beat cream cheese in large bowl with electric mixer at medium speed until fluffy. Beat in brown sugar until smooth. Add eggs, sour cream and vanilla; beat just until blended. Remove 1 cup batter to small bowl; stir in chocolate.

4. Pour plain batter into prepared crust. Drop spoonfuls of chocolate batter over plain batter. Run knife through batters to marbleize. Arrange pecan halves around edge.

5. Bake 50 minutes or until set. Cool completely in pan on wire rack. Cover and refrigerate 2 hours or until ready to serve. Drizzle with caramel topping.

Choco-Berry Cake

MAKES 10 SERVINGS

2 cups Gluten-Free All-Purpose Flour Blend (page 6),* plus additional for pans
1 cup unsweetened cocoa powder
1 cup granulated sugar
1 cup packed brown sugar
2 teaspoons baking powder
1 teaspoon baking soda
1 teaspoon xanthan gum
1 teaspoon espresso powder (optional)
½ teaspoon salt
1½ cups soymilk or other dairy-free milk
½ cup vegetable oil
2 eggs
2 teaspoons vanilla
1 cup semisweet chocolate chips
Fluffy White Frosting (recipe follows)
1 pint strawberries, sliced (about 2 cups), plus additional for garnish

*Or use any all-purpose gluten-free flour blend that does not contain xanthan gum.

1. Preheat oven to 350°F. Grease and flour two 9-inch round cake pans.

2. Combine flour blend, cocoa, granulated sugar, brown sugar, baking powder, baking soda, xanthan gum, espresso powder, if desired, and salt in large bowl.

3. Whisk soymilk, oil, eggs and vanilla in medium bowl. Add to flour mixture; stir until well blended. Stir in chocolate chips. Divide batter between prepared pans.

4. Bake 35 to 45 minutes or until toothpick inserted into centers comes out clean. Cool in pans on wire racks 5 minutes. Remove to wire racks to cool completely.

5. Meanwhile, prepare Fluffy White Frosting. Place one layer on serving plate. Spread with thin layer of frosting. Arrange sliced strawberries over frosting. Top with second layer. Frost top and side of cake. Garnish with additional strawberries.

Fluffy White Frosting: Beat 1½ cups (3 sticks) dairy-free margarine and 1½ teaspoons vanilla in medium bowl with electric mixer at medium speed until light and fluffy. Add 3 cups powdered sugar and ½ teaspoon salt; beat until well blended. Add 3 tablespoons vanilla-flavor creamer; beat until well blended. Gradually add additional 3 cups powdered sugar at low speed. Add additional creamer as needed to make frosting spreadable.

Flourless Dark Chocolate Cake

MAKES 8 TO 10 SERVINGS

16 ounces semisweet baking chocolate, chopped
½ cup (1 stick) butter
4 eggs, at room temperature, separated
¼ cup granulated sugar
2 tablespoons water
½ teaspoon vanilla
½ cup raspberry jam
   Whipped cream (see Tip)

1. Preheat oven to 350°F. Spray 9-inch springform pan with nonstick cooking spray.

2. Melt chocolate and butter in medium saucepan over low heat; stir until well blended. Remove from heat. Add egg yolks, granulated sugar, water and vanilla; mix well.

3. Beat egg whites in large bowl with electric mixer at medium speed. Gradually increase speed to high; beat until stiff peaks form. Fold in one third of chocolate mixture at a time until no white streaks remain. Pour batter into prepared pan; smooth top.

4. Bake 22 to 25 minutes or until center is set. Cool in pan on wire rack 30 minutes.

5. Place raspberry jam in small microwavable bowl; microwave on HIGH 30 seconds or until melted. Drizzle cake with jam and top with whipped cream.

Tip: For whipped cream, beat 1 cup cold whipping cream and 2 tablespoons powdered sugar in large bowl with electric mixer at medium-high speed until soft peaks form.

Polenta Apricot Pudding Cake

MAKES 8 SERVINGS

¼ cup chopped dried apricots
¾ cup sugar
⅔ cup cornmeal
½ cup Gluten-Free All-Purpose Flour Blend (page 6)*
¾ teaspoon xanthan gum
½ teaspoon salt
¼ teaspoon ground nutmeg
1½ cups orange juice
1 cup ricotta cheese
3 tablespoons honey
½ cup slivered almonds

*Or use any all-purpose gluten-free flour blend that does not contain xanthan gum.

1. Preheat oven to 325°F. Spray 9-inch nonstick springform pan with nonstick cooking spray.

2. Place apricots in small bowl; cover with warm water. Let stand 15 minutes to soften. Drain and pat dry.

3. Combine sugar, cornmeal, flour blend, xanthan gum, salt and nutmeg in medium bowl. Beat orange juice, ricotta cheese and honey in large bowl with electric mixer at medium speed 3 minutes or until smooth. Add flour mixture; mix well. Stir in apricots. Pour into prepared pan. Sprinkle with almonds.

4. Bake 40 to 50 minutes or until center is almost set and cake is golden brown. Serve warm.

Carrot-Spice Snack Cake

MAKES 8 SERVINGS

½ cup packed brown sugar

⅓ cup dairy-free margarine

2 eggs

½ cup soymilk or other dairy-free milk

1 teaspoon vanilla

1¼ cups Gluten-Free All-Purpose Flour Blend (page 6)*

¾ cup finely shredded carrots

2 teaspoons baking powder

1½ teaspoons pumpkin pie spice

½ teaspoon xanthan gum

½ teaspoon salt

⅓ cup golden raisins

Powdered sugar

*Or use any all-purpose gluten-free flour blend that does not contain xanthan gum.

1. Preheat oven to 350°F. Spray 8-inch square baking pan with nonstick cooking spray.

2. Beat brown sugar and margarine in medium bowl with electric mixer at medium speed until well blended. Beat in eggs, soymilk and vanilla.

3. Add flour blend, carrots, baking powder, pumpkin pie spice, xanthan gum and salt; beat at low speed until blended. Stir in raisins. Spread batter in prepared pan.

4. Bake 25 to 30 minutes or until toothpick inserted into center comes out clean. Cool completely in pan on wire rack. Sprinkle with powdered sugar just before serving.

Yellow Layer Cake

2 cups Gluten-Free All-Purpose Flour Blend (page 6)*
1¼ teaspoons baking powder
½ teaspoon salt
½ teaspoon xanthan gum
1¼ cups sugar
1 cup (2 sticks) dairy-free margarine
4 eggs
2 teaspoons vanilla
¼ cup soymilk or other dairy-free milk
Dark Chocolate Frosting (recipe follows)

*Or use any all-purpose gluten-free flour blend that does not contain xanthan gum.

1. Preheat oven to 350°F. Spray two 9-inch round cake pans with nonstick cooking spray. Line bottoms with parchment paper.

2. Combine flour blend, baking powder, salt and xanthan gum in medium bowl.

3. Beat sugar and margarine in large bowl with electric mixer at medium speed 8 minutes or until light and fluffy. Add eggs, one at a time, beating well after each addition. Beat in vanilla. Add flour mixture alternately with soymilk, beating at low speed and scraping side and bottom of bowl occasionally. Beat at medium speed 2 minutes. Divide batter between prepared pans. Tap bottoms of pans on counter.

4. Bake 35 to 40 minutes or until toothpick inserted into centers comes out clean. Cool in pans on wire racks 5 minutes. Remove to wire racks to cool completely.

5. Meanwhile, prepare Dark Chocolate Frosting. Fill and frost cake.

Dark Chocolate Frosting

1 cup (2 sticks) dairy-free margarine
3 cups sifted powdered sugar
7 ounces semisweet chocolate, melted
⅓ cup unsweetened cocoa powder
⅔ to 1 cup soy creamer
1½ teaspoons vanilla

continued on page 76

1. Beat margarine in medium bowl with electric mixer at medium speed until light and fluffy. Gradually beat in powdered sugar alternately with melted chocolate and cocoa.

2. Beat in soy creamer by tablespoonfuls until spreadable. Beat in vanilla.

Allergy-Free Strawberry Cake

MAKES 8 SERVINGS

1 package (15 ounces) gluten-free yellow cake mix
½ cup rice milk
½ cup (1 stick) dairy-free margarine
   Prepared powdered egg replacer equal to 3 eggs
2 teaspoons grated lemon peel
1 teaspoon vanilla
1 cup sliced strawberries
1 to 2 tablespoons powdered sugar
4 large strawberries, sliced (optional)

1. Preheat oven to 350°F. Spray 9-inch round cake pan with nonstick cooking spray.

2. Beat cake mix, rice milk, margarine, egg replacer, lemon peel and vanilla in large bowl with electric mixer at low speed 30 seconds. Beat at medium speed 1 minute. Add strawberries; beat at medium speed 1 to 2 minutes or until strawberries are crushed. Spoon batter into prepared pan.

3. Bake 35 to 40 minutes or until golden brown and toothpick inserted into center comes out clean. Cool in pan on wire rack 10 minutes. Remove to wire rack to cool completely. Sprinkle with powdered sugar. Garnish with strawberry slices.

Cupcake Creations

Flourless Chocolate Cupcake Hearts

MAKES 10 CUPCAKES

20 heart-shaped foil baking cups
½ cup (1 stick) butter, cubed
4 ounces bittersweet chocolate, finely chopped
2 tablespoons raspberry liqueur
¾ cup granulated sugar
3 eggs, separated
½ cup unsweetened cocoa powder
  Dash salt
1 package (12 ounces) frozen raspberries, thawed
¼ cup superfine or powdered sugar
  Fresh raspberries (optional)

1. Preheat oven to 350°F. Spray 10 baking cups with nonstick cooking spray. Place each sprayed cup into second unsprayed cup for stability. Arrange cups on rimmed baking sheet.

2. Heat butter and chocolate in medium saucepan over very low heat until melted, stirring frequently. Remove from heat. Stir in raspberry liqueur; set aside to cool slightly.

3. Beat granulated sugar and egg yolks in large bowl with electric mixer at medium speed until light and fluffy. Add chocolate mixture; beat until blended. Sift cocoa into mixture; stir by hand until blended.

4. Beat egg whites and salt in clean large bowl with electric mixer at high speed until stiff peaks form. *Do not overbeat.* Gently fold beaten egg whites into chocolate mixture. Pour batter into prepared cups, filling half full.

5. Bake 10 to 12 minutes or until edges are set and centers are still slightly soft. Remove to wire rack; cool completely. Remove cupcakes from baking cups.

6. Place raspberries in fine mesh strainer over bowl; mash with back of spoon to crush berries and remove seeds. Stir superfine sugar into strained raspberries. To serve, drizzle raspberry sauce on plate; top with cupcake. Garnish with fresh raspberries.

Cherry Pink Cupcakes

MAKES 12 CUPCAKES

1 jar (6 ounces) maraschino cherries
1¼ cups Gluten-Free All-Purpose Flour Blend (page 6)*
1½ teaspoons baking powder
½ teaspoon salt
½ teaspoon xanthan gum
1 cup granulated sugar
2 eggs
½ cup vegetable oil
½ cup soymilk or other dairy-free milk
1 teaspoon vanilla
    Cherry Pink Frosting (recipe follows)
    Additional maraschino cherries (optional)

*Or use any all-purpose gluten-free flour blend that does not contain xanthan gum.

1. Preheat oven to 350°F. Line 12 standard (2½-inch) muffin cups with paper baking cups. Drain cherries, reserving juice for Cherry Pink Frosting. Chop cherries and squeeze out excess moisture. Spread cherries on paper towels to drain. Set aside.

2. Combine flour blend, baking powder, salt and xanthan gum in medium bowl. Beat sugar and eggs in large bowl with electric mixer at medium speed until light and fluffy. Add flour mixture; beat until combined. Add oil, soymilk and vanilla; beat 1 minute or until smooth. Stir in chopped cherries. Spoon batter evenly into prepared muffin cups.

3. Bake 20 minutes or until lightly browned and centers spring back when gently touched. Cool in pan on wire rack 5 minutes. Remove to wire rack to cool completely.

4. Meanwhile, prepare Cherry Pink Frosting; frost cupcakes and garnish with additional cherries.

Cherry Pink Frosting: Beat ½ cup (1 stick) dairy-free margarine in medium bowl with electric mixer at medium speed until light and fluffy. Add 1 cup powdered sugar; beat until blended. Add 4 teaspoons reserved cherry juice and 1 cup powdered sugar; beat until smooth. Add 1 or 2 drops red food coloring for a darker color, if desired. Add additional powdered sugar until frosting is spreadable.

Banana Cupcakes

2 cups Gluten-Free All-Purpose Flour Blend (page 6)*
1½ cups granulated sugar
2 tablespoons packed brown sugar
2 teaspoons baking powder
¾ teaspoon xanthan gum
½ teaspoon salt
½ teaspoon ground cinnamon
¼ teaspoon ground allspice
½ cup vegetable oil
2 eggs
¼ cup soymilk or other dairy-free milk
1 teaspoon vanilla
2 mashed bananas
Chocolate No-Butter Buttercream Frosting (recipe follows)
Gluten-free sprinkles (optional)

*Or use any all-purpose gluten-free flour blend that does not contain xanthan gum.

1. Preheat oven to 350°F. Line 18 standard (2½-inch) muffin cups with paper baking cups.

2. Combine flour blend, granulated sugar, brown sugar, baking powder, xanthan gum, salt, cinnamon and allspice in large bowl. Add oil, eggs, soymilk and vanilla; beat with electric mixer at medium speed 2 minutes or until well blended. Beat in bananas until well blended. Spoon batter evenly into prepared muffin cups.

3. Bake 25 to 30 minutes or until toothpick inserted into centers comes out clean. Cool in pans on wire racks 10 minutes. Remove to wire racks to cool completely.

4. Meanwhile, prepare Chocolate No-Butter Buttercream Frosting; frost cupcakes and decorate with sprinkles, if desired.

Chocolate No-Butter Buttercream Frosting: Beat ½ cup (1 stick) dairy-free margarine in medium bowl with electric mixer at medium speed until light and fluffy. Beat in 2 teaspoons vanilla. Gradually beat in 3½ cups powdered sugar and ½ cup unsweetened cocoa powder. Beat in 4 to 6 tablespoons soy creamer, 1 tablespoon at a time, until frosting is spreadable.

Plum-Side Down Cakes

MAKES 8 CUPCAKES

2 tablespoons dairy-free margarine

3 tablespoons packed brown sugar

3 plums, sliced

1¼ cups Gluten-Free All-Purpose Flour Blend (page 6)*

1½ teaspoons baking powder

½ teaspoon xanthan gum

¼ teaspoon salt

½ cup granulated sugar

2 tablespoons shortening

1 egg

⅓ cup soymilk or other dairy-free milk

½ teaspoon vanilla

Or use any all-purpose gluten-free flour blend that does not contain xanthan gum.

1. Preheat oven to 350°F. Spray 8 standard (2½-inch) muffin cups with nonstick cooking spray.

2. Place margarine in small microwavable bowl. Microwave on LOW (30%) just until melted. Stir in brown sugar. Spoon evenly into prepared muffin cups. Pat plum slices dry and arrange in bottom of each cup.

3. Combine flour blend, baking powder, xanthan gum and salt in small bowl. Beat granulated sugar and shortening in medium bowl with electric mixer at medium speed until fluffy. Beat in egg until well combined. Beat in flour mixture. Add soymilk and vanilla; beat 1 minute or until smooth. Spoon batter evenly into prepared muffin cups; smooth tops. Place pan on baking sheet.

4. Bake 20 to 22 minutes or until toothpick inserted into centers comes out clean. Cool in pan on wire 10 minutes. Run knife around each cup to loosen cakes. Invert onto wire rack to cool completely.

Chocolate Cupcakes

2½ cups Gluten-Free All-Purpose Flour Blend (page 6)*
½ cup unsweetened cocoa powder
1½ teaspoons baking soda
¾ teaspoon xanthan gum
½ teaspoon baking powder
¼ teaspoon salt
1½ cups sugar
3 eggs
½ cup vegetable oil
1 teaspoon vanilla
1¼ cups plain soymilk or other dairy-free milk
Creamy White Frosting (recipe follows)
Gluten-free nonpareils (optional)

Or use any all-purpose gluten-free flour blend that does not contain xanthan gum.

1. Preheat oven to 350°F. Line 18 standard (2½-inch) muffin cups with paper baking cups.

2. Whisk flour blend, cocoa, baking soda, xanthan gum, baking powder and salt in large bowl. Beat sugar, eggs, oil and vanilla in large bowl with electric mixer at medium speed 3 minutes or until thick and smooth. Add flour mixture alternately with soymilk, beating at low speed and scraping side and bottom of bowl occasionally. Beat at medium speed 2 minutes. Spoon batter evenly into prepared muffin cups.

3. Bake 20 to 25 minutes or until toothpick inserted into centers comes out clean. Cool in pans on wire racks 5 minutes. Remove to wire racks to cool completely.

4. Meanwhile, prepare Creamy White Frosting; frost cupcakes and decorate with nonpareils, if desired.

Creamy White Frosting

4 ounces dairy-free cream cheese alternative, at room temperature
3 tablespoons dairy-free margarine, at room temperature
1½ teaspoons vanilla
4 to 5 cups powdered sugar
4 to 6 tablespoons soymilk or other dairy-free milk

continued on page 88

Beat cream cheese alternative and margarine in medium bowl with electric mixer at medium speed until light and fluffy. Beat in vanilla. Gradually beat in powdered sugar. Beat in soymilk by tablespoonfuls until frosting is spreadable.

Mini Chocolate Cheesecakes

MAKES 12 CHEESECAKES

8 ounces semisweet baking chocolate, chopped
3 packages (8 ounces each) cream cheese, softened
½ cup sugar
3 eggs
1 teaspoon vanilla

1. Preheat oven to 325°F. Lightly spray 12 standard (2½-inch) muffin cups with nonstick cooking spray.

2. Place chocolate in 1-cup microwavable bowl. Microwave on HIGH 1 to 1½ minutes or until chocolate is melted, stirring after 1 minute. Let cool slightly.

3. Beat cream cheese and sugar in large bowl with electric mixer at medium speed about 2 minutes or until light and fluffy. Add eggs and vanilla; beat about 2 minutes or until well blended. Beat melted chocolate into cream cheese mixture until well blended.

4. Divide mixture evenly among prepared muffin cups. Place muffin pan in larger baking pan; place on oven rack. Pour warm water into larger pan to depth of ½ to 1 inch.

5. Bake 30 minutes or until edges are dry and centers are almost set. Remove muffin pan from water. Cool cheesecakes completely in muffin pan on wire rack.

Mini Swirl Cheesecakes: Before adding chocolate to cream cheese mixture, place about 2 heaping tablespoonfuls of mixture in each muffin cup. Add chocolate to remaining cream cheese mixture in bowl; beat until well blended. Spoon chocolate mixture on top of plain mixture in muffin cups; swirl with knife before baking.

Sweet Potato Spice Cupcakes

MAKES 18 CUPCAKES

1¼ pounds sweet potatoes, quartered
1½ cups Gluten-Free All-Purpose Flour Blend (page 6)*
1¼ cups granulated sugar
2 teaspoons baking powder
1 teaspoon baking soda
1 teaspoon ground cinnamon
½ teaspoon salt
½ teaspoon xanthan gum
¼ teaspoon ground allspice
¾ cup canola oil
2 eggs
½ cup chopped walnuts or pecans, plus additional for garnish
½ cup raisins
Cream Cheese Frosting (recipe follows)

*Or use any all-purpose gluten-free flour blend that does not contain xanthan gum.

1. Place sweet potatoes in large saucepan; add water to cover by 1 inch. Cover and cook over medium heat 30 minutes or until tender, adding additional water if necessary. Drain sweet potatoes; peel and mash when cool enough to handle. Measure 2 cups.

2. Preheat oven to 325°F. Line 18 standard (2½-inch) muffin cups with paper baking cups.

3. Combine flour blend, granulated sugar, baking powder, baking soda, cinnamon, salt, xanthan gum and allspice in medium bowl. Beat sweet potatoes, oil and eggs in large bowl with electric mixer at low speed until blended. Add flour mixture; beat at medium speed 30 seconds or until well blended. Fold in ½ cup walnuts and raisins. Spoon batter evenly into prepared muffin cups.

4. Bake 25 to 30 minutes or until toothpick inserted into centers comes out clean. Cool completely in pans on wire racks.

5. Meanwhile, prepare Cream Cheese Frosting; frost cupcakes and garnish with additional walnuts.

Cream Cheese Frosting: Beat 1 package (8 ounces) softened cream cheese and ¼ cup (½ stick) softened butter in medium bowl with electric mixer at medium-high speed until creamy. Beat in ¼ teaspoon salt and ¼ teaspoon vanilla. Gradually beat in 1½ cups powdered sugar until well blended. Beat in 1 tablespoon milk at a time until frosting is spreadable.

Fudge Mini Cupcakes

MAKES ABOUT 42 MINI CUPCAKES

¾ cup semisweet chocolate chips
3 tablespoons dairy-free margarine
3 eggs, separated
⅛ teaspoon salt
¼ cup granulated sugar
¼ cup powdered sugar

1. Preheat oven to 300°F. Line 42 mini (1¾-inch) muffin cups with paper baking cups.

2. Melt chocolate chips and margarine in top of double boiler over simmering water. Remove from heat; beat in egg yolks.

3. Beat egg whites and salt in large bowl with electric mixer at medium speed until foamy. Gradually add granulated sugar, beating until stiff peaks form. Fold in chocolate mixture. Spoon batter evenly into prepared muffin cups.

3. Bake 18 minutes or until cupcakes feel firm when very lightly touched. Cool in pans on wire racks 5 minutes. Remove to wire racks to cool completely. (Cupcakes will puff up, but then sink back.) Sprinkle with powdered sugar before serving.

Bars and Brownies

Sweet Potato Coconut Bars

MAKES 16 BARS

30 gluten-free shortbread cookies, crushed

1¼ cups finely chopped walnuts, toasted,* divided

¾ cup flaked coconut, divided

¼ cup (½ stick) butter, softened

2 cans (16 ounces each) sweet potatoes, well drained and mashed (2 cups)

2 eggs

1 teaspoon ground cinnamon

½ teaspoon ground ginger

¼ to ½ teaspoon ground cloves

¼ teaspoon salt

1 can (14 ounces) sweetened condensed milk

¾ cup gluten-free butterscotch chips**

*To toast walnuts, spread in single layer on ungreased baking sheet. Bake in preheated 350°F oven 8 to 10 minutes or until golden brown, stirring frequently.

**Read labels carefully as not all butterscotch chips are gluten-free.

1. Preheat oven to 350°F.

2. Combine cookie crumbs, 1 cup walnuts, ½ cup coconut and butter in food processor; pulse until well combined. Press two thirds of mixture onto bottom of 8-inch square baking pan.

3. Beat sweet potatoes, eggs, cinnamon, ginger, cloves and salt in large bowl with electric mixer at medium-low speed until well blended. Gradually add sweetened condensed milk; beat until well blended. Spoon filling evenly over prepared crust. Top with remaining crumb mixture, pressing lightly.

4. Bake 45 to 50 minutes or until knife inserted into center comes out clean. Sprinkle with butterscotch chips, remaining ¼ cup walnuts and ¼ cup coconut. Bake 5 minutes. Cool completely in pan on wire rack. Cover and refrigerate 2 hours before serving.

Tip: Cookies can be crushed in a food processor or in a resealable food storage bag with a rolling pin or meat mallet.

Double Chocolate Brownies

MAKES 16 BROWNIES

¼ cup soy flour
¼ cup cornstarch
½ teaspoon baking soda
¼ teaspoon salt
½ cup (1 stick) butter
1 cup packed brown sugar
½ cup unsweetened cocoa powder
2 eggs
½ cup semisweet chocolate chips
1 teaspoon vanilla

1. Preheat oven to 350°F. Spray 8-inch square baking pan with nonstick cooking spray.

2. Combine soy flour, cornstarch, baking soda and salt in small bowl; mix well.

3. Melt butter in large saucepan over low heat. Add brown sugar; cook and stir until sugar is dissolved. Remove from heat; sift in cocoa and stir until combined. Stir in flour mixture until smooth. (Mixture will be thick.)

4. Add eggs; beat until smooth and well blended. Stir in chocolate chips and vanilla. Pour batter into prepared pan.

5. Bake 25 to 30 minutes or until toothpick inserted into center comes out almost clean.

Cherry Cheesecake Swirl Bars

MAKES 16 BARS

Crust

1⅔ cups gluten-free shortbread cookie crumbs
½ cup (1 stick) butter, melted
¼ cup sugar

Cheesecake

2 packages (8 ounces each) cream cheese, softened
½ cup sugar
3 eggs
½ cup sour cream
½ teaspoon almond extract
3 tablespoons cherry preserves, melted and strained

1. Preheat oven to 325°F.

2. Combine cookie crumbs, butter and ¼ cup sugar in medium bowl; mix well. Press mixture onto bottom of 9-inch square baking pan. Bake 10 minutes or until set but not browned. Cool completely.

3. Beat cream cheese in medium bowl with electric mixer at medium speed until fluffy. Add ½ cup sugar; beat until smooth. Add eggs, one at a time, beating well after each addition. Add sour cream and almond extract; beat until well blended. Spread evenly over prepared crust.

4. Drizzle melted preserves in zigzag pattern over cheesecake batter. Drag tip of knife through jam and batter to make swirls.

5. Place baking pan in larger baking dish; add water to come halfway up sides of cheesecake.

6. Bake 45 to 50 minutes or until knife inserted 1 inch from edge comes out clean. Cool completely in pan on wire rack. Cover and refrigerate 2 hours or until ready to serve.

Caramel Chocolate Chunk Blondies

MAKES 24 BLONDIES

1½ cups Gluten-Free All-Purpose Flour Blend (page 6)*
1 teaspoon baking powder
½ teaspoon xanthan gum
½ teaspoon salt
¾ cup granulated sugar
¾ cup packed brown sugar
½ cup (1 stick) dairy-free margarine
2 eggs
1½ teaspoons vanilla
1½ cups semisweet chocolate chunks
⅓ cup caramel ice cream topping

*Or use any all-purpose gluten-free flour blend that does not contain xanthan gum.

1. Preheat oven to 350°F. Spray 13×9-inch baking pan with nonstick cooking spray.

2. Combine flour blend, baking powder, xanthan gum and salt in medium bowl. Beat granulated sugar, brown sugar and margarine in large bowl with electric mixer at medium speed until smooth and creamy. Beat in eggs and vanilla until well blended. Add flour mixture; beat at low speed until blended. Stir in chocolate chunks.

3. Spread batter evenly in prepared pan. Drop spoonfuls of caramel topping over batter; swirl into batter with knife.

4. Bake 25 minutes or until golden brown. Cool completely in pan on wire rack.

Lemon Bars

MAKES 16 BARS

1 cup Gluten-Free All-Purpose Flour Blend (page 6)*
1 cup macadamia nuts or slivered almonds
½ cup (1 stick) cold butter, cut into pieces
½ cup powdered sugar, plus additional for garnish
1 tablespoon plus 1 teaspoon grated lemon peel, divided
½ teaspoon salt
1 cup granulated sugar
3 eggs
⅓ cup lemon juice

*Or use any all-purpose gluten-free flour blend that does not contain xanthan gum.

1. Preheat oven to 350°F. Spray 9-inch square baking pan with nonstick cooking spray.

2. Combine flour blend, nuts, butter, powdered sugar, 1 teaspoon lemon peel and salt in food processor; process until mixture forms fine crumbs. Press mixture onto bottom of prepared pan. Bake 15 minutes or until light golden brown.

3. Beat granulated sugar, eggs, lemon juice and remaining 1 tablespoon lemon peel in large bowl with electric mixer at medium speed until blended. Pour evenly over warm crust.

4. Bake 18 to 20 minutes or until center is set and edges are golden brown. Cool completely in pan on wire rack. Sprinkle with additional powdered sugar. Store tightly covered at room temperature.

Rocky Road Brownies

MAKES 16 BROWNIES

⅔ cup Gluten-Free All-Purpose Flour Blend (page 6)*
½ teaspoon salt
½ teaspoon baking powder
½ teaspoon xanthan gum
½ cup (1 stick) dairy-free margarine
½ cup unsweetened cocoa powder
1 cup sugar
2 eggs
¼ cup soymilk or other dairy-free milk
2 teaspoons vanilla
1 cup mini marshmallows
1 cup coarsely chopped walnuts
1 cup semisweet chocolate chips

*Or use any all-purpose gluten-free flour blend that does not contain xanthan gum.

1. Preheat oven to 350°F. Spray 8-inch square baking pan with nonstick cooking spray.

2. Combine flour blend, salt, baking powder and xanthan gum in small bowl. Combine margarine and cocoa in large saucepan over low heat, stirring constantly until smooth. Remove from heat; whisk in sugar, eggs, soymilk and vanilla until smooth. Stir in flour mixture until well blended. Pour batter into prepared pan.

3. Bake 25 to 35 minutes or until center feels dry. Sprinkle with marshmallows, walnuts and chocolate chips. Bake 3 to 5 minutes or until topping is slightly melted. Cool in pan on wire rack.

Butterscotch Toffee Gingersnap Squares

MAKES 24 BARS

40 gluten-free gingersnap cookies
6 tablespoons (¾ stick) butter, melted
1 cup butterscotch chips*
½ cup pecan pieces
½ cup chopped peanuts
½ cup milk chocolate toffee bits
½ cup mini semisweet chocolate chips
1 can (14 ounces) sweetened condensed milk
1½ teaspoons vanilla

Read labels carefully as not all butterscotch chips are gluten-free.

1. Preheat oven to 350°F. Line 13×9-inch baking pan with foil, leaving 1-inch overhang. Spray with nonstick cooking spray.

2. Place cookies in food processor; process until crumbs form. Measure 2 cups.

3. Combine 2 cups crumbs and butter in medium bowl; mix well. Press mixture evenly onto bottom of prepared pan. Bake 4 to 5 minutes or until light brown around edges.

4. Meanwhile, combine butterscotch chips, pecans, peanuts, toffee bits and chocolate chips in medium bowl. Whisk condensed milk and vanilla in small bowl; pour over warm crust. Sprinkle with butterscotch mixture, pressing down gently.

5. Bake 15 to 18 minutes or until golden and bubbly. Cool completely in pan on wire rack. Remove from pan using foil; cut into bars.

Cocoa Bottom Banana Pecan Bars

MAKES 24 BARS

1 cup sugar

½ cup (1 stick) butter, softened

5 ripe bananas, mashed

1 egg

1 teaspoon vanilla

1½ cups Gluten-Free All-Purpose Flour Blend (page 6)*

1 teaspoon baking powder

1 teaspoon baking soda

½ teaspoon xanthan gum

½ teaspoon salt

½ cup chopped pecans

¼ cup unsweetened cocoa powder

*Or use any all-purpose gluten-free flour blend that does not contain xanthan gum.

1. Preheat oven to 350°F. Spray 13×9-inch baking pan with nonstick cooking spray.

2. Beat sugar and butter in large bowl with electric mixer at medium speed until creamy. Add bananas, egg and vanilla; beat until well blended. Combine flour blend, baking powder, baking soda, xanthan gum and salt in medium bowl. Add to banana mixture; beat until well blended. Stir in pecans.

3. Remove half of batter to another bowl; stir in cocoa. Spread chocolate batter in prepared pan. Top with plain batter; swirl gently with knife.

4. Bake 30 to 35 minutes or until edges are lightly browned. Cool completely in pan on wire rack. Cut into bars.

Chewy Corn Bread Cookies

MAKES 4 DOZEN COOKIES

1 cup (2 sticks) butter, softened
⅔ cup plus 2 tablespoons sugar, divided
1 egg
1 teaspoon vanilla
½ teaspoon salt
2 cups corn flour
½ cup instant polenta

1. Beat butter and ⅔ cup sugar in large bowl with electric mixer at medium-high speed until creamy. Beat in egg, vanilla and salt until well blended. Combine corn flour and polenta in medium bowl. Gradually add to butter mixture, beating well after each addition. (Dough will be very sticky.)

2. Shape dough into two discs. Wrap in plastic wrap; refrigerate at least 2 hours.

3. Preheat oven to 350°F. Line cookie sheets with parchment paper.

4. Shape dough into 1-inch balls. Roll in remaining 2 tablespoons sugar. Place 1 inch apart on prepared cookie sheets.

5. Bake 12 to 14 minutes or until bottoms are lightly browned. Cool completely on cookie sheets.

Orange Snickerdoodles

MAKES ABOUT 3 DOZEN COOKIES

½ cup (1 stick) dairy-free margarine, softened
1 cup granulated sugar
1 tablespoon grated orange peel
1 egg
¾ teaspoon vanilla, divided
1½ cups Gluten-Free All-Purpose Flour Blend (page 6)*
¾ teaspoon xanthan gum
½ teaspoon baking soda
½ teaspoon cream of tartar
¼ cup orange-colored sugar or granulated sugar
1 cup powdered sugar
2 tablespoons orange juice

*Or use any all-purpose gluten-free flour blend that does not contain xanthan gum.

1. Beat margarine in large bowl with electric mixer at medium speed 30 seconds. Add granulated sugar and orange peel; beat 1 minute. Beat in egg and ½ teaspoon vanilla until well blended. Add flour blend, xanthan gum, baking soda and cream of tartar; beat just until combined. Cover with plastic wrap; refrigerate 1 hour.

2. Preheat oven to 375°F. Line cookie sheets with parchment paper.

3. Shape dough into 1-inch balls; roll in orange-colored sugar. Place balls 2 inches apart on prepared cookie sheets.

4. Bake 12 to 15 minutes or until edges are lightly browned. Cool on cookie sheets on wire racks 5 minutes.

5. For icing, whisk powdered sugar, orange juice and remaining ¼ teaspoon vanilla in small bowl until smooth. Add additional powdered sugar or juice if necessary.

6. Gently loosen cookies from parchment but leave on cookie sheets. Drizzle icing over warm cookies with fork. Remove cookies to wire racks to cool completely. Store in airtight container.

Flourless Peanut Butter Cookies

1 cup packed brown sugar
1 cup creamy peanut butter
1 egg
½ cup semisweet chocolate chips

1. Preheat oven to 350°F.

2. Beat brown sugar, peanut butter and egg in large bowl with electric mixer at medium speed until blended and smooth. Shape dough into 24 (1½-inch) balls. Place 2 inches apart on ungreased cookie sheets. Flatten dough slightly with fork and press 3 to 4 chocolate chips into top of each cookie.

3. Bake 10 to 12 minutes or until set. Remove to wire racks to cool completely.

Variation: Instead of topping cookies with chocolate chips, melt the chocolate chips. Drizzle melted chocolate over cooled cookies and let stand until set.

Choco-Coco Pecan Crisps

MAKES ABOUT 6 DOZEN COOKIES

1½ cups Gluten-Free All-Purpose Flour Blend (page 6)*
1 cup chopped pecans
⅓ cup unsweetened cocoa powder
½ teaspoon baking soda
½ teaspoon xanthan gum
1 cup packed brown sugar
½ cup (1 stick) butter, softened
1 egg
1 teaspoon vanilla
1 cup flaked coconut

*Or use any all-purpose gluten-free flour blend that does not contain xanthan gum.

1. Combine flour blend, pecans, cocoa, baking soda and xanthan gum in small bowl. Beat brown sugar and butter in large bowl with electric mixer at medium speed until light and fluffy. Beat in egg and vanilla. Add flour mixture, blending until stiff dough forms.

2. Sprinkle coconut on work surface. Divide dough into four pieces. Shape each piece into log about 1½ inches in diameter; roll in coconut until thickly coated. Wrap in plastic wrap; refrigerate until firm, at least 1 hour or up to 2 weeks. (For longer storage, freeze up to 6 weeks.)

3. Preheat oven to 350°F. Cut logs into ⅛-inch-thick slices. Place 2 inches apart on ungreased cookie sheets.

4. Bake 10 to 13 minutes or until firm. Remove to wire racks to cool completely.

Graham Crackers

MAKES ABOUT 1 DOZEN CRACKERS

½ cup sweet rice flour (mochiko),* plus additional for work surface
½ cup sorghum flour
½ cup packed brown sugar
⅓ cup tapioca flour
½ teaspoon baking soda
½ teaspoon salt
¼ cup (½ stick) butter or dairy-free margarine
2 tablespoons plus 2 teaspoons whole milk or soymilk
2 tablespoons honey
1 tablespoon vanilla

Sweet rice flour is usually labeled mochiko (the Japanese term). It is available in the Asian section of large supermarkets, at Asian grocers and online.

1. Combine ½ cup sweet rice flour, sorghum flour, brown sugar, tapioca flour, baking soda and salt in food processor; pulse to combine, making sure brown sugar is free of lumps. Add butter; pulse until coarse crumbs form.

2. Whisk milk, honey and vanilla in small bowl or measuring cup until well blended and honey is dissolved. Pour into flour mixture; process until dough forms. (Dough will be very soft and sticky.)

3. Pat into dough into rectangle on floured surface. Wrap in plastic wrap; refrigerate at least 4 hours or up to 2 days.

4. Preheat oven to 325°F. Cover work surface with parchment paper; generously dust with rice flour.

5. Roll dough to ⅛-inch-thick rectangle on parchment paper using rice-floured rolling pin. (If dough becomes too sticky, return to refrigerator or freezer for several minutes.) Place dough on parchment paper on baking sheet. Score dough into cracker shapes (do not cut all the way through). Prick dough in rows with tines of fork. Place baking sheet in freezer 5 to 10 minutes or in refrigerator 15 to 20 minutes.

6. Bake chilled crackers 25 minutes or until firm and slightly darkened. Slide crackers on parchment onto wire rack to cool. Cut along score lines when cooled slightly.

Serving Suggestion: Serve crackers as a snack or for s'mores with chocolate and marshmallows.

One-Bite Pineapple Chewies

MAKES ABOUT 1½ DOZEN COOKIES

½ cup whipping cream
¼ cup sugar
⅛ teaspoon salt
1 cup finely chopped dried pineapple
½ cup chopped slivered almonds
¼ cup mini semisweet chocolate chips
¼ cup white rice flour

1. Preheat oven to 350°F. Line cookie sheets with parchment paper.

2. Stir cream, sugar and salt in large bowl until sugar dissolves. Stir in pineapple, almonds and chocolate chips. Stir in rice flour until blended. Drop dough by rounded teaspoonfuls about 1 inch apart onto prepared cookie sheets.

3. Bake 13 to 15 minutes or until edges are golden brown. Cool on cookie sheets 2 minutes. Remove to wire racks to cool completely.

Sunflower Seed Butter Cookies

MAKES ABOUT 1 DOZEN COOKIES

1 cup creamy sunflower seed butter*
1 cup sugar
1 egg
1 teaspoon vanilla
½ cup mini chocolate chips

*Do not use "natural" sunflower seed butter that separates.

1. Preheat oven to 350°F. Line cookie sheet with parchment paper.

2. Beat sunflower seed butter, sugar, egg and vanilla in large bowl with electric mixer at medium speed until smooth. Stir in chocolate chips. Drop dough by tablespoonfuls onto prepared cookie sheet. Flatten cookies in criss-cross pattern with fork.

3. Bake 10 to 12 minutes or until firm. *Do not overbake.* Cool on cookie sheet 2 minutes. Remove to wire rack to cool completely.

Chocolate Sandwich Cookies

¾ cup (1½ sticks) dairy-free margarine, divided
1 package (15 ounces) gluten-free chocolate cake mix
4 to 5 tablespoons vanilla rice milk, divided
1 egg
3 tablespoons unsweetened cocoa powder, divided
1 tablespoon tapioca flour
1½ cups powdered sugar
Marshmallow creme (optional)

1. Preheat oven to 350° F. Line cookie sheets with parchment paper. Melt ½ cup margarine in small saucepan over low heat.

2. Beat cake mix, melted margarine, 2 tablespoons rice milk, egg, 1 tablespoon cocoa and tapioca flour in large bowl with electric mixer at medium speed 1 minute or blended and dough comes together. Add additional 1 tablespoon rice milk, if necessary.

3. Shape dough by level tablespoonfuls into balls; place 1 inch apart on prepared cookie sheet.

4. Bake 10 minutes. (Cookies will puff up and be very delicate.) Cool on cookie sheets 10 minutes. Remove to wire racks to cool completely.

5. For chocolate filling, beat remaining ¼ cup margarine, 2 tablespoons cocoa, 2 tablespoons rice milk and powdered sugar in large bowl with electric mixer at high speed until light and fluffy, scraping down bowl occasionally.

6. Spread scant tablespoon chocolate filling or marshmallow creme on half of cookies; top with remaining cookies.

Lemony Arrowroot Cookies

MAKES 1 DOZEN COOKIES

¼ cup (½ stick) butter, softened

⅓ cup granulated sugar

1 egg

Grated peel and juice of 1 lemon

½ teaspoon vanilla

1¼ cups Gluten-Free All-Purpose Flour Blend (page 6),* plus additional
for work surface

½ cup arrowroot

½ teaspoon baking powder

¼ teaspoon salt

¼ cup powdered sugar

1 teaspoon grated lemon peel, plus additional for garnish

1 tablespoon lemon juice, plus additional if necessary

Or use any all-purpose gluten-free flour blend that does not contain xanthan gum.

1. Preheat oven to 350°F. Grease cookie sheet.

2. Beat butter and granulated sugar in large bowl with electric mixer at medium speed until creamy. Add egg, grated peel and juice of 1 lemon and vanilla; beat until well blended. Add 1¼ cups flour blend, arrowroot, baking powder and salt; beat at low speed just until combined.

3. Roll out dough on floured surface to ⅛-inch thickness. Cut out shapes with cookie cutters. Place on prepared cookie sheet.

4. Bake 8 to 10 minutes. (Cookies will not brown.) Remove to wire rack to cool completely.

5. For glaze, combine powdered sugar and 1 teaspoon lemon peel in small bowl; stir in enough lemon juice to make pourable glaze. Drizzle glaze over cookies. Garnish with additional lemon peel.

Cocoa Raisin-Chip Cookies

MAKES ABOUT 4 DOZEN COOKIES

1½ cups Gluten-Free All-Purpose Flour Blend (page 6)*
¼ cup unsweetened cocoa powder
1 teaspoon baking powder
½ teaspoon salt
¼ teaspoon xanthan gum
1 cup packed brown sugar
½ cup granulated sugar
½ cup (1 stick) dairy-free margarine
½ cup shortening
2 eggs
1 teaspoon vanilla
1½ cups dairy-free semisweet chocolate chips
1 cup raisins
¾ cup chopped walnuts

*Or use any all-purpose gluten-free flour blend that does not contain xanthan gum.

1. Preheat oven to 350°F. Line cookie sheets with parchment paper.

2. Combine flour blend, cocoa, baking powder, salt and xanthan gum in medium bowl. Beat brown sugar, granulated sugar, margarine and shortening in large bowl with electric mixer at medium speed until light and fluffy. Add eggs, one at a time, beating well after each addition. Beat in vanilla. Add flour mixture; beat until well blended. Stir in chocolate chips, raisins and walnuts. Drop dough by tablespoonfuls onto prepared cookie sheets.

3. Bake 10 to 12 minutes or until set. Remove to wire racks to cool completely.

Crispy Toffee Cookies

MAKES ABOUT 4 DOZEN COOKIES

½ cup rice flour
½ cup dry roasted peanuts
⅛ teaspoon salt
½ cup packed brown sugar
⅓ cup dairy-free margarine
¼ cup light corn syrup
1 teaspoon vanilla
¼ cup chocolate chips, melted (optional)

1. Preheat oven to 375°F. Line two cookie sheets with parchment paper.

2. Combine rice flour, peanuts and salt in food processor; process until mixture resembles coarse crumbs.

3. Combine brown sugar, margarine and corn syrup in medium saucepan; bring to a boil over medium heat, stirring frequently. Remove from heat; stir in peanut mixture and vanilla until well blended. Return pan to low heat to keep batter warm and pliable. Spoon six rounded ½ teaspoonfuls of batter 3 inches apart on one prepared cookie sheet.

4. Bake exactly 4 minutes. While cookies are baking, spoon batter on second cookie sheet. When cookies have baked 4 minutes, immediately remove from oven. (Cookies will have very light color and will appear not to be completely baked.) Slide cookies on parchment paper onto wire rack to cool completely.

5. While second batch of cookies is baking, line first cookie sheet with new sheet of parchment paper; continue to prepare and bake cookies in batches of six. (Sheets of parchment paper can be reused after cookies are removed.) Peel cookies from parchment paper; remove to wire rack.

6. Drizzle melted chocolate over cookies, if desired; let stand until set. Store cookies in airtight container with parchment paper or waxed paper between layers to prevent sticking.

Pies, Crisps and More

Hidden Pumpkin Pies

MAKES 6 SERVINGS

1½ **cups solid-pack pumpkin**
1 **cup evaporated milk**
2 **eggs**
½ **cup sugar**
1¼ **teaspoons vanilla, divided**
1 **teaspoon pumpkin pie spice***
3 **egg whites**
¼ **teaspoon cream of tartar**
⅓ **cup honey**

Or substitute ½ teaspoon ground cinnamon, ¼ teaspoon ground ginger and ⅛ teaspoon each ground allspice and ground nutmeg for 1 teaspoon pumpkin pie spice.

1. Preheat oven to 350°F.

2. Combine pumpkin, evaporated milk, eggs, sugar, 1 teaspoon vanilla and pumpkin pie spice in large bowl; mix well. Pour into six 6-ounce custard cups or soufflé dishes. Place in shallow baking dish or pan. Pour boiling water around custard cups to depth of 1 inch. Bake 25 minutes or until set.

3. Meanwhile, beat egg whites, cream of tartar and remaining ¼ teaspoon vanilla in medium bowl with electric mixer at high speed until soft peaks form. Gradually add honey, beating until stiff peaks form.

4. Spread egg white mixture over tops of hot pumpkin pies. Bake 8 to 12 minutes or until meringue is golden brown. Let stand 10 minutes. Serve warm.

Mixed Berry Crisp

MAKES ABOUT 9 SERVINGS

6 cups mixed berries, thawed if frozen
¾ cup packed brown sugar, divided
¼ cup quick-cooking tapioca
   Juice of ½ lemon
1 teaspoon ground cinnamon
½ cup rice flour
6 tablespoons cold butter or dairy-free margarine, cut into small pieces
½ cup sliced almonds

1. Preheat oven to 375°F. Spray 8- or 9-inch square baking pan with nonstick cooking spray.

2. Combine berries, ¼ cup brown sugar, tapioca, lemon juice and cinnamon in large bowl. Pour into prepared pan.

3. Combine rice flour, remaining ½ cup brown sugar and butter in food processor; pulse until mixture resembles coarse crumbs. Add almonds; pulse until combined. (Leave some large pieces of almonds.) Sprinkle over berries.

4. Bake 20 to 30 minutes or until topping is golden brown.

Caramel Chocolate Tart

MAKES 8 SERVINGS

Crust

¾ cup Gluten-Free All-Purpose Flour Blend (page 6),* plus additional
for work surface

¾ cup unsweetened cocoa powder

½ cup (1 stick) cold butter, cubed

3 tablespoons sugar

½ teaspoon xanthan gum

⅛ teaspoon salt

3 tablespoons whipping cream

1 egg

1 egg yolk

Filling

1 cup sugar

¼ cup water

2 tablespoons light corn syrup

5 tablespoons butter

¼ cup whipping cream

1 teaspoon vanilla

Ganache

½ cup plus 1 tablespoon whipping cream

4 ounces bittersweet chocolate, chopped

Fresh raspberries (optional)

Or use any all-purpose gluten-free flour blend that does not contain xanthan gum.

1. For crust, beat ¾ cup flour blend, cocoa, ½ cup butter, 3 tablespoons sugar, xanthan gum and salt in large bowl with electric mixer at medium speed until mixture resembles coarse crumbs. Beat in 3 tablespoons cream, egg and egg yolk just until combined. Wrap in plastic wrap; refrigerate at least 1 hour or up to 3 days.

2. Roll dough into 10-inch circle (about ¼ inch thick) on floured surface. Press into 9-inch tart pan. Trim edges to fit pan. Prick bottom with fork. Cover and refrigerate 30 minutes.

3. Preheat oven to 350°F. Line tart shell with foil and fill with pie weights or dried beans. Bake 15 minutes.

continued on page 136

4. Remove foil and weights. Bake 10 to 12 minutes. Remove to wire rack to cool completely.

5. For filling, combine 1 cup sugar, water and corn syrup in large saucepan; cook and stir over medium-high heat until sugar is completely melted and mixture is deep amber in color. Remove from heat. Whisk in 5 tablespoons butter, ¼ cup cream and vanilla. Let stand 5 minutes to cool slightly. Pour into crust. Let stand 45 minutes or until set.

6. For ganache, combine ½ cup plus 1 tablespoon cream in small saucepan; bring to a simmer. Place chocolate in large bowl. Whisk cream into chocolate until smooth and well blended.

7. Pour ganache over filling, tilting pan to cover completely. Refrigerate 2 hours or until set. Garnish with raspberries.

Apple Pie

MAKES 6 TO 8 SERVINGS

Pie Crust For Double Crust Pie (page 144)
6 medium apples, such as Gala, Jonathon or Granny Smith, peeled and cut into
   ¼-inch slices
¾ cup sugar
½ cup dried cranberries
2 tablespoons cornstarch or tapioca flour
2 teaspoons lemon juice
1 teaspoon ground cinnamon

1. Prepare Pie Crust. Preheat oven to 425°F. Grease 9-inch pie pan.

2. Press one crust into prepared pan. Combine apples, sugar, cranberries, cornstarch, lemon juice and cinnamon in large bowl; gently toss. Arrange evenly in prepared crust.

3. Place remaining crust over filling. Pinch edges of crust together; trim excess pastry. Cut slits in top of crust to allow steam to vent.

4. Bake 12 minutes. *Reduce oven temperature to 350°F.* Bake 30 to 40 minutes. Cool completely in pan on wire rack.

Pumpkin-Pineapple Pie

MAKES 8 SERVINGS

Graham Cracker Crust (recipe follows)
1 can (8 ounces) pineapple rings in juice, undrained
2 tablespoons powdered egg replacer
1 can (15 ounces) solid-pack pumpkin
1 can (14 ounces) sweetened condensed milk
1 teaspoon ground cinnamon
1 teaspoon ground nutmeg
½ teaspoon ground ginger
⅛ teaspoon salt
1 tablespoon butter
Whipped cream (optional)

1. Preheat oven to 350°F. Prepare Graham Cracker Crust; bake 8 minutes or until browned. Cool completely. Drain pineapple; reserve ¼ cup juice. Set aside four pineapple rings; reserve remaining pineapple for another use.

2. Beat egg replacer and ¼ cup reserved pineapple juice in medium bowl with electric mixer at low speed until smooth. Add pumpkin, sweetened condensed milk, cinnamon, nutmeg, ginger and salt; beat until fluffy. Pour into prepared crust.

3. Bake 45 to 50 minutes or until center is set. Cool completely in pan on wire rack.

4. Meanwhile, melt butter in small skillet over medium heat. Add pineapple rings; cook and stir until lightly golden. Cool completely.

5. Cut pineapple rings in half; arrange on pie. Top with whipped cream, if desired.

Graham Cracker Crust

25 gluten-free graham crackers, broken into small pieces
¾ cup (1½ sticks) butter, cubed
⅓ cup sugar

1. Spray deep-dish 10-inch pie pan with nonstick cooking spray.

2. Place graham crackers in food processor; pulse until finely crushed. Add butter and sugar; process until well combined. Press mixture firmly onto bottom and up side of prepared pan.

Banana-Coconut Cream Pie

MAKES 8 SERVINGS

Crust
1 cup almonds
1 tablespoon sugar
½ cup flaked coconut
¼ cup (½ stick) butter, cut into pieces
Pinch salt

Filling
2 bananas
1 teaspoon lemon juice
½ cup sugar
¼ cup cornstarch
¼ teaspoon salt
3 cups whole milk
2 egg yolks
1 teaspoon vanilla

Topping
1 banana
2 tablespoons flaked coconut, toasted*
Whipped cream

To toast coconut, spread in single layer in small heavy skillet. Cook over medium heat 1 to 2 minutes, stirring frequently, until lightly browned. Immediately remove from skillet. Cool before using.

1. Preheat oven to 350°F. Spray 9-inch pie pan with nonstick cooking spray.

2. Place almonds and 1 tablespoon sugar in food processor; pulse until almonds are ground. Add ½ cup coconut; pulse to combine. Add butter and pinch of salt; pulse until mixture begins to stick together. Press mixture onto bottom and up side of prepared pan. Bake 10 to 12 minutes or until edge is golden brown. Cool completely.

3. Slice two bananas; sprinkle with lemon juice. Arrange on bottom of prepared crust.

4. Combine ½ cup sugar, cornstarch and ¼ teaspoon salt in medium saucepan. Whisk milk and egg yolks in medium bowl until well blended; slowly stir into sugar mixture. Cook and stir over medium heat until thickened. Bring to a boil; boil 1 minute. Remove from heat; stir in vanilla.

continued on page 142

5. Pour mixture over bananas in crust. Cover and refrigerate at least 2 hours or until ready to serve.

6. Slice remaining banana; arrange on top of pie. Sprinkle with toasted coconut and top with whipped cream.

Cranberry Pear Cobbler

MAKES 8 SERVINGS

3 pounds ripe pears (6 pears), peeled and sliced
1½ cups fresh or frozen cranberries
¼ cup plus 1½ tablespoons granulated sugar, divided
1 tablespoon cornstarch
1 tablespoon grated orange peel
1 teaspoon ground cinnamon
1 package (about 15 ounces) gluten-free yellow cake mix
1 cup buttermilk
½ cup (1 stick) butter, softened
2 teaspoons vanilla
1½ tablespoons packed brown sugar
Whipped cream (optional)

1. Preheat oven to 400°F. Spray 13×9-inch baking dish with nonstick cooking spray.

2. Combine pears, cranberries, ¼ cup granulated sugar, cornstarch, orange peel and cinnamon in large bowl; toss to coat. Pour into prepared baking dish.

3. Bake 20 minutes or until bubbly.

4. Meanwhile, beat cake mix, buttermilk, butter and vanilla in large bowl with electric mixer at low speed 30 seconds or until moistened. Beat at medium speed 2 minutes. Remove baking dish from oven. Pour topping evenly over fruit. Sprinkle with brown sugar and remaining 1½ tablespoons granulated sugar.

5. Bake 30 to 35 minutes or until topping is golden brown. Serve warm with whipped cream, if desired.

Pecan Pie

MAKES 8 SERVINGS

Pie Crust (recipe follows)
3 eggs
¾ cup dark corn syrup
¾ cup sugar
1 teaspoon vanilla
¼ teaspoon salt
2 cups chopped pecans

1. Prepare Pie Crust. Preheat oven to 425°F.

2. Beat eggs in large bowl. Add corn syrup, sugar, vanilla and salt; beat until well blended. Pour into crust; sprinkle evenly with pecans. Bake 45 to 50 minutes or until set. Cool completely in pan on wire rack.

Pie Crust

1 cup Gluten-Free All-Purpose Flour Blend (page 6),* plus additional
    for work surface
2 tablespoons rice flour
1½ teaspoons sugar
½ teaspoon xanthan gum
¼ teaspoon salt
6 tablespoons (¾ stick) cold butter, cubed
1 egg
2 teaspoons cider vinegar

*Or use any all-purpose gluten-free flour blend that does not contain xanthan gum.

1. Combine flour blend, rice flour, sugar, xanthan gum and salt in medium bowl; mix well. Cut in butter with pastry blender or two knives until mixture forms coarse crumbs. Make a well in center of flour mixture. Add egg and vinegar; stir just until dough forms. (If dough is dry, add 1 tablespoon cold water at a time until dough sticks together when pressed). Shape into flat disc. Wrap in plastic wrap; refrigerate at least 45 minutes.

2. Spray 9-inch pie pan with nonstick cooking spray. Roll out dough into 11-inch circle on lightly floured surface; place in prepared pan. Flute edge as desired.

For Double Crust Pie: Double all ingredients and shape dough into two flat discs. For top crust, roll out second disc slightly larger than pie pan.

Holiday Treats

Holiday Cut-Out Cookies

MAKES ABOUT 2 DOZEN COOKIES

2 cups Gluten-Free All-Purpose Flour Blend (page 6)*
1 teaspoon xanthan gum
1 teaspoon ground cinnamon
½ teaspoon salt
½ teaspoon baking powder
¾ cup granulated sugar
½ cup shortening
1 egg
2 to 3 tablespoons milk, plus additional if necessary
2 teaspoons vanilla
1 container (16 ounces) white frosting
Assorted food coloring
Assorted colored sugar and sprinkles

*Or use any all-purpose gluten-free flour blend that does not contain xanthan gum.

1. Combine flour blend, xanthan gum, cinnamon, salt and baking powder in medium bowl. Beat sugar and shortening in large bowl with electric mixer at medium speed 2 minutes or until light and fluffy. Beat in egg. Gradually beat in flour mixture. Beat in 2 tablespoons milk and vanilla. Add additional milk by teaspoonfuls if dough is too dry. Shape dough into two discs. Wrap in plastic wrap; refrigerate 15 minutes.

2. Preheat oven to 350°F. Line cookie sheets with parchment paper.

3. Roll out dough between sheets of waxed paper. Cut out shapes with cookie cutters. Place on prepared cookie sheets.

4. Bake 8 to 10 minutes or until edges begin to brown. Remove to wire racks to cool completely.

5. Divide frosting among several bowls. Add food coloring to each bowl, a few drops at a time, until desired shades are reached. Frost cookies and decorate with colored sugars and sprinkles.

Pink Peppermint Meringues

MAKES ABOUT 6 DOZEN MERINGUES

3 egg whites
⅛ teaspoon peppermint extract
5 drops red food coloring
½ cup superfine sugar*
6 peppermint candies, finely crushed

Or use ½ cup granulated sugar processed in food processor 1 minute until very fine.

1. Preheat oven to 200°F. Line cookie sheets with parchment paper.

2. Beat egg whites in medium bowl with electric mixer at medium-high speed 45 seconds or until foamy. Beat in peppermint extract and food coloring. Beat in sugar, 1 tablespoon at a time, until egg whites are stiff and glossy. Drop meringue by teaspoonfuls into 1-inch mounds on prepared cookie sheets; sprinkle evenly with crushed candies.

3. Bake 2 hours or until meringues are dry when tapped. Slide parchment paper with meringues onto wire racks to cool completely.

Chocolate Gingersnaps

MAKES ABOUT 3 DOZEN COOKIES

¾ cup sugar
1 package (15 ounces) gluten-free chocolate cake mix
1 tablespoon ground ginger
2 eggs
⅓ cup vegetable oil

1. Preheat oven to 350°F. Spray cookie sheets with nonstick cooking spray. Place sugar in shallow bowl.

2. Combine cake mix and ginger in large bowl. Add eggs and oil; stir until well blended. Shape tablespoonfuls of dough into 1-inch balls; roll in sugar to coat. Place 2 inches apart on prepared cookie sheets.

3. Bake 10 minutes or until set. Cool on cookie sheets 2 minutes. Remove to wire racks to cool completely.

Gingerbread

MAKES 16 SERVINGS

2 cups Gluten-Free All-Purpose Flour Blend (page 6)*
2 teaspoons ground ginger
¾ teaspoon xanthan gum
½ teaspoon baking powder
½ teaspoon baking soda
½ teaspoon salt
½ teaspoon ground cinnamon
1 cup ginger ale
¾ cup packed brown sugar
½ cup molasses
2 eggs
6 tablespoons (¾ stick) butter, melted and cooled
1 tablespoon grated fresh ginger
Whipped cream (optional)

*Or use any all-purpose gluten-free flour blend that does not contain xanthan gum.

1. Preheat oven to 350°F. Spray 9-inch square baking pan with nonstick cooking spray.

2. Combine flour blend, ground ginger, xanthan gum, baking powder, baking soda, salt and cinnamon in medium bowl. Whisk ginger ale, brown sugar, molasses, eggs, butter and fresh ginger in large bowl until well blended. Add flour mixture in two additions, stirring until well blended after each addition. Pour batter into prepared pan.

3. Bake 30 to 35 minutes or until toothpick inserted into center comes out clean. Cool in pan 10 minutes. Remove to wire rack to cool slightly. Serve warm or at room temperature with whipped cream, if desired.

Golden Kolacky

MAKES ABOUT 2½ DOZEN COOKIES

1 cup Gluten-Free All-Purpose Flour Blend (page 6),* plus additional
   for work surface
½ teaspoon xanthan gum
½ cup (1 stick) butter, softened
4 ounces cream cheese, softened
   Fruit preserves

*Or use any all-purpose gluten-free flour blend that does not contain xanthan gum.

1. Combine 1 cup flour blend and xanthan gum in small bowl. Beat butter and cream cheese in large bowl with electric mixer at medium speed until smooth. Gradually add flour mixture, beating until soft dough forms. Divide dough in half; shape into two discs. Wrap in plastic wrap; refrigerate 1 hour or until firm.

2. Preheat oven to 375°F. Roll out dough to ⅛-inch thickness on floured surface. Cut into 2½-inch squares. Spoon 1 teaspoon preserves into center of each square. Bring up two opposite corners to center; pinch together tightly to seal. Fold sealed tip to one side; press to seal. Place 1 inch apart on ungreased cookie sheets.

3. Bake 10 to 15 minutes or until lightly browned. Remove to wire racks to cool completely.

Shortbread Cookies

1½ cups Gluten-Free All-Purpose Flour Blend (page 6)*
½ cup sweet rice flour (mochiko)
1 teaspoon xanthan gum
1 cup (2 sticks) butter, softened
½ cup powdered sugar
2 tablespoons packed brown sugar
¼ teaspoon salt
Colored sugars (optional)

*Or use any all-purpose gluten-free flour blend that does not contain xanthan gum.

1. Whisk flour blend, sweet rice flour and xanthan gum in medium bowl. Beat butter, powdered sugar, brown sugar and salt in large bowl with electric mixer at medium speed 2 minutes or until light and fluffy. Add flour mixture, ½ cup at a time, beating well after each addition. Shape dough into 14-inch-long log. If desired, roll in colored sugars. Wrap in plastic wrap; refrigerate 1 hour.**

2. Preheat oven to 300°F. Cut log into ½-inch-thick slices; place on ungreased cookie sheets.

3. Bake 20 to 25 minutes or until lightly browned. Cool on cookie sheets 5 minutes. Remove to wire racks to cool completely.

**The dough can be stored in the refrigerator for up to two days or in the freezer for up to one month. If frozen, thaw the dough in the refrigerator overnight before slicing and baking.

Tip: For square cookies, shape the dough log into a square before rolling in colored sugar.

Fruit Cake

MAKES 12 SERVINGS

2 cups Gluten-Free All-Purpose Flour Blend (page 6),* plus additional for pan
1½ teaspoons xanthan gum
1 teaspoon baking powder
1 teaspoon ground cinnamon
1 teaspoon grated fresh ginger
½ teaspoon baking soda
½ teaspoon salt
½ teaspoon ground cloves
2 cups packed dark brown sugar
1 cup (2 sticks) butter, softened
6 eggs
½ cup orange juice
¼ cup molasses
2 cups golden raisins
1½ cups chopped dried apricots
1 cup chopped walnuts
1 cup chopped pecans
1 cup dried cranberries
Powdered sugar (optional)

*Or use any all-purpose gluten-free flour blend that does not contain xanthan gum.

1. Preheat oven to 300°F. Spray 12-cup (10-inch) bundt pan with nonstick cooking spray. Dust with flour blend. Combine 2 cups flour blend, xanthan gum, baking powder, cinnamon, ginger, baking soda, salt and cloves in medium bowl.

2. Beat brown sugar and butter in large bowl with electric mixer at medium-high speed 3 minutes or until light and fluffy. Add eggs, one at a time, beating at medium speed until well blended after each addition. Add orange juice and molasses; beat at low speed until well blended. Gradually add flour mixture; beat at medium speed 2 minutes. Fold in raisins, apricots, walnuts, pecans and cranberries. Pour batter into prepared pan.

3. Bake 2 to 2½ hours or until toothpick inserted near center comes out clean.** Cool in pan on wire rack 1 hour. Remove to wire rack to cool completely. Sprinkle with powdered sugar just before serving, if desired.

**If cake becomes too dark on top, tent loosely with foil for last 30 to 60 minutes of baking time.

Almond Crescents

1 cup (2 sticks) butter, softened
⅓ cup sugar
1¾ cups Gluten-Free All-Purpose Flour Blend (page 6)*
¼ cup cornstarch
1 teaspoon vanilla
½ teaspoon xanthan gum
1½ cups ground toasted almonds**
Chocolate Glaze (recipe follows)

*Or use any all-purpose gluten-free flour blend that does not contain xanthan gum.

**To toast almonds, spread in single layer on baking sheet. Bake in preheated 350°F oven 8 to 10 minutes or until golden brown, stirring frequently.

1. Preheat oven to 325°F.

2. Beat butter and sugar in large bowl with electric mixer at medium speed until creamy. Beat in flour blend, cornstarch, vanilla and xanthan gum. Beat in almonds. Shape tablespoonfuls of dough into crescents. Place 2 inches apart on ungreased cookie sheets.

3. Bake 22 to 25 minutes or until lightly browned. Cool on cookie sheets 1 minute. Remove to wire racks to cool completely.

4. Prepare Chocolate Glaze; drizzle over cookies.

Chocolate Glaze: Place ½ cup semisweet chocolate chips and 1 tablespoon butter in small resealable bag. Place bag in bowl of hot water for 2 to 3 minutes or until chocolate is softened. Dry bag with paper towel. Knead until chocolate mixture is smooth. Cut off very tiny corner of bag.

Apricot-Cranberry Holiday Bread

MAKES ABOUT 16 SERVINGS

> 2 cups Gluten-Free All-Purpose Flour Blend (page 6),* plus additional for pan
> ½ cup dried apricots, chopped
> ½ cup dried cranberries, chopped
> 3 tablespoons orange juice
> ⅔ cup plus ¼ cup warm water (110°F), divided
> 1 package (¼ ounce) active dry yeast
> 3 tablespoons sugar, divided
> 1½ teaspoons xanthan gum
> ½ teaspoon salt
> ½ teaspoon ground ginger
> ¼ teaspoon ground nutmeg
> 5 tablespoons butter, melted and cooled slightly
> 3 eggs, at room temperature
> ½ cup chopped toasted pecans**

*Or use any all-purpose gluten-free flour blend that does not contain xanthan gum.

**To toast pecans, spread in a single layer on ungreased baking sheet. Bake in preheated 350°F oven 8 to 10 minutes or until fragrant, stirring occasionally.

1. Spray 9-inch square baking pan with nonstick cooking spray; dust with flour blend.

2. Combine apricots, cranberries and orange juice in small microwavable bowl. Cover and microwave on HIGH 25 to 35 seconds to soften; set aside. Combine ¼ cup warm water, yeast and 1 tablespoon sugar in large bowl; let stand 10 minutes or until foamy.

3. Add 2 cups flour blend, remaining 2 tablespoons sugar, xanthan gum, salt, ginger and nutmeg to yeast mixture. Whisk butter, remaining ⅔ cup warm water and eggs in small bowl until well blended. Gradually beat into flour mixture with electric mixer at low speed until well blended. Scrape side of bowl; beat at medium-high speed 3 minutes or until well blended.

4. Drain apricot mixture; pat dry. Fold apricot mixture and pecans into batter. Pour into prepared pan. Cover and let rise in warm place 1 hour or until batter almost reaches top of pan.

5. Preheat oven to 350°F. Bake 35 to 40 minutes or until toothpick inserted into center comes out clean. Cool in pan on wire rack 10 minutes. Remove to wire rack to cool completely.

Chocolate Peppermint Macaroons

MAKES 2 DOZEN COOKIES

4 ounces bittersweet chocolate, chopped (½ cup)

2 squares (1 ounce each) unsweetened baking chocolate

2 egg whites, at room temperature

⅛ teaspoon salt

½ cup sugar

½ teaspoon peppermint extract

2¾ cups flaked coconut

½ cup finely crushed peppermint candies*

About 18 peppermint candies will yield ½ cup finely crushed peppermints. To crush, place unwrapped candy in a heavy-duty resealable plastic food storage bag. Loosely seal the bag, leaving an opening for air to escape. Crush with a rolling pin, meat mallet or the bottom of a heavy skillet.

1. Line cookie sheets with parchment paper or spray with nonstick cooking spray.

2. Place bittersweet and unsweetened chocolate in medium microwavable bowl. Microwave on HIGH at 30-second intervals, stirring between each interval, until melted and smooth. Cool 15 minutes.

3. Preheat oven to 325°F. Beat egg whites and salt in large bowl with electric mixer at high speed until soft peaks form. Gradually add sugar, beating until stiff peaks form. Add chocolate; beat at low speed just until blended. Stir in peppermint extract. Fold in coconut until blended, scraping down side of bowl.

4. Shape level tablespoonfuls of batter into 1-inch balls; place 2 inches apart on prepared cookie sheets. Make small indentation in center; fill with crushed candy.

5. Bake 12 minutes or until set. Outsides should be crisp and insides should be moist and chewy. Remove to wire racks to cool completely.

Gingerbread People

MAKES ABOUT 2 DOZEN COOKIES

1 cup sorghum flour
1 cup white rice flour, plus additional for work surface
¼ cup tapioca flour
2 teaspoons baking soda
1 teaspoon salt
1 teaspoon xanthan gum
1 teaspoon ground ginger
½ teaspoon ground allspice
½ teaspoon ground cinnamon
½ cup (1 stick) butter, softened
½ cup packed brown sugar
⅓ cup molasses
1 egg
   Assorted gluten-free icings and/or candies

1. Combine sorghum flour, rice flour, tapioca flour, baking soda, salt, xanthan gum, ginger, allspice and cinnamon in large bowl.

2. Beat butter and brown sugar in large bowl with electric mixer at medium speed until creamy. Add molasses and egg; beat until well blended. Gradually add flour mixture, beating at low speed until dough forms. Shape dough into disc. Wrap in plastic wrap; refrigerate 2 hours or until firm.

3. Preheat oven to 350°F. Line cookie sheets with parchment paper. Roll out dough to ⅛-inch thickness on lightly rice-floured surface. Cut out shapes with cookie cutters. Place 2 inches apart on prepared cookie sheets.

4. Bake 10 to 15 minutes or until set. Remove to wire racks to cool completely. Decorate as desired. Store in airtight containers.

Thumbprint Cookies

MAKES 2 DOZEN COOKIES

1 cup (2 sticks) butter, softened

½ cup packed dark brown sugar

2 eggs, separated

2 teaspoons vanilla

2 cups Gluten-Free All-Purpose Flour Blend (page 6)*

½ teaspoon salt

2¼ cups chopped walnuts

¼ cup raspberry jam

Or use any all-purpose gluten-free flour blend that does not contain xanthan gum.

1. Preheat oven to 375°F. Line cookie sheets with parchment paper.

2. Beat butter and brown sugar in large bowl with electric mixer at medium-high speed 2 minutes or until light and fluffy. Add egg yolks and vanilla; beat at low speed, scraping side of bowl occasionally. Beat in flour blend and salt just until combined.

3. Whisk egg whites in shallow dish. Place walnuts in separate shallow dish. Roll tablespoonfuls of dough into balls; dip in egg whites and roll in walnuts to coat. Place on prepared cookie sheets. Make small indentation in center of each ball with thumb or back of small spoon. Fill with jam.

4. Bake 12 to 15 minutes or until golden brown and filling is set, rotating cookie sheets halfway through baking time. Cool on cookie sheets 5 minutes. Remove to wire racks to cool completely.

Sour Cream Cranberry Coffee Cake

MAKES 24 SERVINGS

Cake

2½ cups Gluten-Free All-Purpose Flour Blend (page 6)*

2 teaspoons baking powder

1½ teaspoons xanthan gum

1 teaspoon baking soda

1 teaspoon unflavored gelatin

½ teaspoon salt

1½ cups granulated sugar

¾ cup (1½ sticks) butter

3 eggs

1 cup sour cream

2 teaspoons vanilla

2 cup fresh or frozen cranberries (do not thaw frozen berries)

Streusel

½ cup packed brown sugar

¼ cup Gluten-Free All-Purpose Flour Blend (page 6)*

¾ teaspoon ground cinnamon

¼ teaspoon ground nutmeg

¼ teaspoon salt

3 tablespoons cold butter, cubed

*Or use any all-purpose gluten-free flour blend that does not contain xanthan gum.

1. Preheat oven to 350°F. Spray 13×9-inch baking pan with nonstick cooking spray.

2. Combine 2½ cups flour blend, baking powder, xanthan gum, baking soda, gelatin and ½ teaspoon salt in medium bowl.

3. Beat granulated sugar and ¾ cup butter in large bowl with electric mixer at medium-high speed until light and fluffy. Add eggs, one at a time, beating well at medium speed after each addition. Beat in sour cream and vanilla; scrape side of bowl. Add flour mixture in two additions; beat at low speed until well blended. Fold in cranberries. Pour batter into prepared pan.

4. Bake 40 minutes. Meanwhile for streusel, combine brown sugar, ¼ cup flour blend, cinnamon, nutmeg and ¼ teaspoon salt in small bowl. Cut in 3 tablespoons butter with pastry blender or two knives until mixture resembles coarse crumbs. Sprinkle streusel evenly over cake. Bake 10 minutes or until toothpick inserted into center comes out clean. Serve warm or at room temperature.

Crispy, Crunchy, Chewy

Chocolate Coconut Almond Macaroons

MAKES 1½ DOZEN COOKIES

1⅓ cups flaked coconut
⅔ cup sugar
2 egg whites
½ teaspoon vanilla
¼ teaspoon almond extract
   Pinch salt
4 ounces sliced almonds, coarsely crushed
18 whole almonds
   Chocolate Ganache (recipe follows)

1. Combine coconut, sugar, egg whites, vanilla, almond extract and salt in medium bowl; mix well. Fold in sliced almonds. Cover and refrigerate at least 1 hour or overnight.

2. Preheat oven to 350°F. Line cookie sheets with parchment paper.

3. Shape tablespoonfuls of dough into balls. Place 1 inch apart on prepared cookie sheet. Press one whole almond into center of each cookie.

4. Bake 15 minutes or until lightly browned. Cool on cookie sheets 5 minutes. Remove to wire racks to cool completely.

5. Meanwhile, prepare Chocolate Ganache. Dip bottom of each cookie into ganache. Place cookies on clean parchment or waxed paper-lined cookie sheet. Refrigerate until ganache is set. Store covered in refrigerator.

Chocolate Ganache: Place ½ cup semisweet chocolate chips in shallow bowl. Heat ¼ cup whipping cream in small saucepan over low heat until bubbles form around edge. Pour cream over chocolate; let stand 5 minutes. Stir until smooth. Let cool 10 to 15 minutes.

Cocoa Chewies

⅓ cup powdered sugar

2 tablespoons flaked coconut

2 tablespoons unsweetened cocoa powder

1 tablespoon cornstarch

3 egg whites

½ teaspoon vanilla

¼ cup granulated sugar

1. Preheat oven to 250°F. Line cookie sheets with parchment paper or foil.

2. Combine powdered sugar, coconut, cocoa and cornstarch in small bowl. Beat egg whites and vanilla in medium bowl with electric mixer at high speed until foamy. Gradually add granulated sugar, 1 tablespoon at a time, beating until stiff peaks form. Gently fold in coconut mixture. Pipe or spoon batter into scant 2-inch stars or mounds on prepared cookie sheets.

3. Bake 1 hour. Cool cookies completely on cookie sheets.

Pistachio Macarons

⅓ cup unsalted shelled pistachios (1½ ounces)
1½ cups powdered sugar
⅔ cup blanched almond flour*
3 egg whites, at room temperature**
Green paste food coloring
¼ cup granulated sugar
Chocolate Ganache or Pistachio Filling (page 176)

*Almond flour, also called almond powder, is available in the specialty flour section of the supermarket or can be ordered online.

**For best results, separate the eggs while cold. Leave the egg whites at room temperature for 3 or 4 hours. Reserve yolks in refrigerator for another use.

1. Line two baking sheets with parchment paper; place another sheet underneath each to protect macarons from burning or cracking. (Do not use insulated baking sheets.)

2. Place pistachios in food processor; pulse about 1 minute or until coarsely ground. Add powdered sugar and almond flour; pulse 2 to 3 minutes or until ground into very fine powder, scraping bowl occasionally. Sift mixture twice; discard any remaining large pieces.

3. Beat egg whites in large bowl with electric mixer at high speed until foamy. Add food coloring. Gradually add granulated sugar; beat at high speed 2 to 3 minutes or until stiff, shiny peaks form, scraping bowl occasionally.

4. Add half of pistachio mixture to egg whites. Stir with spatula to combine (about 12 strokes). Repeat with remaining pistachio mixture. Mix 15 strokes more by pressing against side of bowl and scooping from bottom until batter is smooth and shiny. (Check consistency by dropping spoonful of batter onto plate. It should have a peak which quickly relaxes back into batter. Do not overmix or undermix.)

5. Attach ½-inch plain piping tip to pastry bag. Scoop batter into bag. Pipe 1-inch circles about 2 inches apart onto prepared baking sheets. Tap baking sheets on flat surface to remove air bubbles. Let rest, uncovered, until tops harden slightly, about 15 minutes on dry days to 1 hour in more humid conditions. Gently touch top of macaron to check. When batter does not stick, macarons are ready to bake.

continued on page 176

Pistachio Macarons, continued

6. Meanwhile, preheat oven to 375°F.* Place rack in center of oven. Place one sheet of macarons in oven. Bake 5 minutes. *Reduce oven temperature to 325°F.* Bake 10 to 13 minutes, checking at 5-minute intervals. If macarons begin to brown, cover loosely with foil and reduce oven temperature or prop oven door open slightly. Repeat with remaining macarons.

7. Cool completely on baking sheet on wire rack. While cooling, if cookies appear to be sticking to parchment, lift parchment edges and spray baking sheet lightly with water. (Steam will help release macarons.)

8. Meanwhile, prepare Chocolate Ganache or Pistachio Filling. Match same size cookies; spread bottom macaron with filling and top with another. Store macarons in covered container in refrigerator up to 5 days. Freeze for longer storage.

Oven temperature is crucial. Use an oven thermometer, if possible.

Chocolate Ganache: Place 4 ounces chopped semisweet chocolate in shallow bowl. Heat ½ cup whipping cream in small saucepan over low heat until bubbles form around edge. Pour cream over chocolate; let stand 5 minutes. Stir until smooth.

Pistachio Filling: Combine 1 cup powdered sugar and ⅓ cup shelled pistachios in food processor; process 2 to 3 minutes or until coarse paste forms, scraping bowl occasionally. Add 6 tablespoons softened butter and ½ teaspoon vanilla; pulse to combine.

Peanut Meringue Cookies

MAKES ABOUT 3 DOZEN COOKIES

4 egg whites
½ teaspoon cream of tartar
1 cup sugar
¼ cup ground peanuts

1. Preheat oven to 250°F. Line cookie sheets with parchment paper.

2. Beat egg whites in large bowl with electric mixer at medium-high speed until foamy. Add cream of tartar; beat until soft peaks form. Gradually add sugar; beat until stiff peaks form. Fold in peanuts. Drop batter by teaspoonfuls onto prepared cookie sheets.

3. Bake 20 minutes or until lightly browned. Remove to wire racks to cool completely.

Chocolate Macarons

1 cup powdered sugar
⅔ cup blanched almond flour*
3 tablespoons unsweetened cocoa powder
3 egg whites, at room temperature**
¼ cup granulated sugar
Chocolate Ganache (page 176), chocolate-hazelnut spread or raspberry jam

*Almond flour, also called almond powder, is available in the specialty flour section of the supermarket or can be ordered online.

**For best results, separate the eggs while cold. Leave the egg whites at room temperature for 3 or 4 hours. Reserve yolks in refrigerator for another use.

1. Line two baking sheets with parchment paper; place another sheet underneath each to protect macarons from burning or cracking. (Do not use insulated baking sheets.)

2. Place powdered sugar, almond flour and cocoa in food processor. Pulse 2 to 3 minutes or until ground into very fine powder, scraping bowl occasionally. Sift mixture twice; discard any remaining large pieces.

3. Beat egg whites in large bowl with electric mixer at high speed until foamy. Gradually add granulated sugar, beating at high speed 2 to 3 minutes or until stiff, shiny peaks form, scraping bowl occasionally.

4. Add half of flour mixture to egg whites. Stir with spatula to combine (about 12 strokes). Repeat with remaining flour mixture. Mix about 15 strokes more by pressing against side of bowl and scooping from bottom until batter is smooth and shiny. (Check consistency by dropping spoonful of batter onto plate. It should have a peak which quickly relaxes back into batter. Do not overmix or undermix.)

5. Attach ½-inch plain piping tip to pastry bag. Scoop batter into bag. Pipe 1-inch circles about 2 inches apart onto prepared baking sheet. Tap baking sheets on flat surface to remove air bubbles. Let macarons rest, uncovered, until tops harden slightly, about 15 minutes on dry days to 1 hour in more humid conditions. Gently touch top of macaron to check. When batter does not stick, macarons are ready to bake.

continued on page 180

Chocolate Macarons, continued

6. Meanwhile, preheat oven to 375°F.* Place rack in center of oven. Place one sheet of macarons in oven. Bake 5 minutes. *Reduce oven temperature to 325°F.* Bake 10 to 13 minutes, checking at 5-minute intervals. If macarons begin to brown, cover loosely with foil and reduce oven temperature or prop oven open slightly. Repeat with remaining macarons.

7. Cool completely on baking sheet on wire rack. While cooling, if cookies appear to be sticking to parchment, lift parchment edges and spray baking sheet lightly with water. (Steam will help release macarons.)

8. Meanwhile, prepare Chocolate Ganache. Match same size cookies; spread bottom macaron with ganache and top with another. Store macarons in covered container in refrigerator up to 5 days. Freeze for longer storage.

Oven temperature is crucial. Use an oven thermometer, if possible.

Coconut Meringues

MAKES 2 DOZEN COOKIES

3 egg whites
¼ teaspoon cream of tartar
⅛ teaspoon salt
¾ cup sugar
2¼ cups flaked coconut, toasted*
1 teaspoon vanilla

To toast coconut, spread evenly on baking sheet. Bake in preheated 350°F oven 5 to 7 minutes or until light golden brown, stirring occasionally. Cool before using.

1. Preheat oven to 300°F. Line cookie sheets with parchment paper or foil.

2. Beat egg whites, cream of tartar and salt in large bowl with electric mixer at high speed until soft peaks form. Beat in sugar, 1 tablespoon at a time, until stiff, shiny peaks form. Fold in coconut and vanilla. Drop batter by tablespoonfuls 2 inches apart onto prepared cookie sheets; flatten slightly.

3. Bake 18 to 22 minutes or until golden brown. Cool on cookie sheets 1 minute. Remove to wire racks to cool completely. Store in airtight container.

Sesame and Red Bean Macarons

MAKES ABOUT 1 DOZEN COOKIES

1⅓ cups powdered sugar, divided
½ cup plus 2 tablespoons almond flour
2 egg whites, at room temperature
5 tablespoons granulated sugar
2 teaspoons sesame seeds
4 ounces cream cheese, softened
¼ cup red bean paste**

*Almond flour, also called almond powder, is available in the specialty flour section of the supermarket or can be ordered online.

**Red bean paste may be found in Asian specialty markets or it can be ordered online.

1. Line two baking sheets with parchment paper. Combine 1 cup powdered sugar and almond flour in food processor. Pulse into fine powder, scraping bowl occasionally. Sift mixture into medium bowl; discard large pieces.

2. Beat egg whites in large bowl with electric mixer at high speed until foamy. Gradually add granulated sugar; beat at high speed 2 to 3 minutes or until stiff, shiny peaks form, scraping bowl occasionally.

3. Add half of flour mixture to egg whites. Stir with spatula to combine (about 12 strokes). Repeat with remaining flour mixture. Mix about 15 strokes more by pressing against side of bowl and scooping from bottom until batter is smooth and shiny. Check consistency by dropping spoonful of batter onto plate. It should have a peak which quickly relaxes back into batter. Do not overmix or undermix.

4. Attach ½-inch plain tip to piping bag. Scoop batter into bag. Pipe 1-inch circles about 2 inches apart onto prepared baking sheets. Tap baking sheets on flat surface to remove air bubbles. Sprinkle half of cookies with sesame seeds. Let macarons rest, uncovered, until tops harden slightly, about 15 minutes on dry days to 1 hour in more humid conditions. Gently touch top of macaron to check. When batter does not stick, macarons are ready to bake.

5. Meanwhile, preheat oven to 350°F. Place rack in center of oven. Bake 15 to 18 minutes, rotating baking sheets halfway through baking time. Cool completely on baking sheets. When cooling, if cookies appear to be sticking to parchment, lift parchment edges and spray baking sheet lightly with water. (Steam will help release cookies.)

continued on page 184

Crispy, Crunchy, Chewy

6. For filling, beat cream cheese, red bean paste and remaining ⅓ cup powdered sugar in large bowl with electric mixer at medium speed about 1 minute or until smooth.

7. Match same size cookies, one each plain and sesame; pipe or spread filling on flat side of plain cookie and top with sesame cookie.

Mexican Chocolate Macaroons

MAKES ABOUT 3 DOZEN COOKIES

8 squares (1 ounce each) semisweet chocolate, divided
1¾ cups plus ⅓ cup whole almonds, divided
¾ cup sugar
2 egg whites
1 teaspoon ground cinnamon
1 teaspoon vanilla

1. Preheat oven to 400°F. Spray cookie sheets with nonstick cooking spray or line with parchment paper.

2. Place 5 chocolate squares in food processor; process until coarsely chopped. Add 1¾ cups almonds and sugar; pulse until finely ground. Add egg whites, cinnamon and vanilla; process just until mixture forms moist dough.

3. Shape dough into 1-inch balls. (Dough will be sticky.) Place 2 inches apart on prepared cookie sheets. Press one whole almond into center of each cookie.

4. Bake 8 to 10 minutes or just until set. Cool on cookie sheets 2 minutes. Remove to wire racks to cool completely.

5. Chop remaining 3 chocolate squares; place in small resealable food storage bag. Microwave on HIGH 1 minute; knead bag. Microwave at additional 30-second intervals until chocolate is melted, kneading after each interval. Cut off tiny corner of bag. Drizzle chocolate over cookies. Let stand until set. Store in airtight container.

Dutch Chocolate Meringues

MAKES ABOUT 6 DOZEN COOKIES

¼ cup finely chopped pecans
2½ tablespoons unsweetened Dutch process cocoa powder
3 egg whites
¼ teaspoon salt
¾ cup granulated sugar
Powdered sugar (optional)

1. Preheat oven to 200°F. Line cookie sheets with foil; spray foil with nonstick cooking spray.

2. Combine pecans and cocoa in medium bowl.

3. Beat egg whites and salt in large bowl with electric mixer at high speed until light and foamy. Gradually beat in granulated sugar until stiff peaks form. Gently fold pecan mixture into egg white mixture with rubber spatula by gently cutting down to bottom of bowl, scraping up side of bowl, then folding over top of mixture. Repeat until pecan mixture is evenly incorporated.

4. Spoon batter into pastry bag fitted with large plain tip. Pipe 1-inch mounds 2 inches apart onto prepared cookie sheets.

5. Bake 1 hour. Turn oven off. Do not open oven door. Let stand in oven 2 hours to overnight or until set.

6. Carefully peel cookies from foil. Sprinkle with powdered sugar, if desired. Store loosely covered at room temperature up to 2 days.

Meringue Mushrooms: Pipe same number of 1-inch-tall "stems" as mounds. Bake as directed in step 5. When cookies are firm, attach "stems" to "caps" with melted chocolate. Sprinkle with sifted cocoa.

Metric Conversion Chart

VOLUME MEASUREMENTS (dry)

$\frac{1}{8}$ teaspoon = 0.5 mL
$\frac{1}{4}$ teaspoon = 1 mL
$\frac{1}{2}$ teaspoon = 2 mL
$\frac{3}{4}$ teaspoon = 4 mL
1 teaspoon = 5 mL
1 tablespoon = 15 mL
2 tablespoons = 30 mL
$\frac{1}{4}$ cup = 60 mL
$\frac{1}{3}$ cup = 75 mL
$\frac{1}{2}$ cup = 125 mL
$\frac{2}{3}$ cup = 150 mL
$\frac{3}{4}$ cup = 175 mL
1 cup = 250 mL
2 cups = 1 pint = 500 mL
3 cups = 750 mL
4 cups = 1 quart = 1 L

VOLUME MEASUREMENTS (fluid)

1 fluid ounce (2 tablespoons) = 30 mL
4 fluid ounces ($\frac{1}{2}$ cup) = 125 mL
8 fluid ounces (1 cup) = 250 mL
12 fluid ounces (1$\frac{1}{2}$ cups) = 375 mL
16 fluid ounces (2 cups) = 500 mL

WEIGHTS (mass)

$\frac{1}{2}$ ounce = 15 g
1 ounce = 30 g
3 ounces = 90 g
4 ounces = 120 g
8 ounces = 225 g
10 ounces = 285 g
12 ounces = 360 g
16 ounces = 1 pound = 450 g

DIMENSIONS

$\frac{1}{16}$ inch = 2 mm
$\frac{1}{8}$ inch = 3 mm
$\frac{1}{4}$ inch = 6 mm
$\frac{1}{2}$ inch = 1.5 cm
$\frac{3}{4}$ inch = 2 cm
1 inch = 2.5 cm

OVEN TEMPERATURES

250°F = 120°C
275°F = 140°C
300°F = 150°C
325°F = 160°C
350°F = 180°C
375°F = 190°C
400°F = 200°C
425°F = 220°C
450°F = 230°C

BAKING PAN SIZES

Utensil	Size in Inches/Quarts	Metric Volume	Size in Centimeters
Baking or Cake Pan (square or rectangular)	8×8×2	2 L	20×20×5
	9×9×2	2.5 L	23×23×5
	12×8×2	3 L	30×20×5
	13×9×2	3.5 L	33×23×5
Loaf Pan	8×4×3	1.5 L	20×10×7
	9×5×3	2 L	23×13×7
Round Layer Cake Pan	8×1½	1.2 L	20×4
	9×1½	1.5 L	23×4
Pie Plate	8×1¼	750 mL	20×3
	9×1¼	1 L	23×3
Baking Dish or Casserole	1 quart	1 L	—
	1½ quart	1.5 L	—
	2 quart	2 L	—